Healing Emotional Wounds

Healing
Emotional
Wounds

*A Story of Overcoming
the Long Hard Road to
Recovery from Abuse
and Abandonment*

Nancy M. Welch

NEW YORK

Healing Emotional Wounds

A Story of Overcoming the Long Hard Road to
Recovery from Abuse and Abandonment

Published in New York, New York, by Morgan James Publishing. Morgan James and The Entrepreneurial Publisher are trademarks of Morgan James, LLC.
www.MorganJamesPublishing.com

The Morgan James Speakers Group can bring authors to your live event. For more information or to book an event visit The Morgan James Speakers Group at www.TheMorganJamesSpeakersGroup.com.

BitLit
FOR ALL THE BOOKS YOU OWN

FREE eBook edition for your
existing eReader with purchase

PRINT NAME ABOVE

For more information,
instructions, restrictions, and
to register your copy, go to
www.bitlit.ca/readers/register
or use your QR Reader to scan
the barcode:

ISBN 978-1-61448-696-1 paperback
ISBN 978-1-61448-697-8 eBook
ISBN 978-1-61448-698-5 audio
ISBN 978-1-61448-872-9 hard cover
Library of Congress Control Number:
2013945998

Photographer:
Nancy M.Welch

Cover Design by:
Chris Treccani
www.3dogdesign.net

Interior Design by:
Bonnie Bushman
bonnie@caboodlegraphics.com

In an effort to support local communities, raise awareness and funds, Morgan James Publishing donates a percentage of all book sales for the life of each book to Habitat for Humanity Peninsula and Greater Williamsburg.

Get involved today, visit
www.MorganJamesBuilds.com.

Habitat
for Humanity®
Peninsula and
Greater Williamsburg
Building Partner

To Alyona and Alec, who discovered the light
beyond the darkness of humanity and thrived,
and to my mother, who showed me the power
of love and faith

"….We are called to act with justice,
we are called to love tenderly;
we are called to serve one another,
to walk humbly with God."

Table of Contents

Acknowledgements

I first need to thank my editor, Earl, who patiently and wisely guided me through revisions to make our story more readable and meaningful. And my siblings (Ed, Ben, Robbie and Ruth) and their spouses who never lost faith in the children and were always there to love and support us through many challenges; by so doing they modeled a strong family and what it means to care for, and help each other, no matter what. I want to personally thank Aleta, my assistant and dear friend, who knew the right words of encouragement, when hugs were needed, masterfully managed my professional schedule throughout chaos and who at all times was a gentle, caring presence whom the children absolutely adore. Numerous members of Emmanuel Episcopal Church (many are specifically mentioned in the book) provided direct assistance, kept Alyona's mailbox full at The Bridges, took the children into their homes when I had professional commitments, gave me strength and tenacity to endure and truly accepted, without reservation, my belief that we were called to be a family. I will try to name them all but offer apologies for those whom I may have unintentionally forgotten – John, Ann, Sarah, Ashley, Pat, Rich, Karen, Silvio, Mary Pehlam, Lewis, Lucy, Roger, Liz, Mary Lou, Terry, Marti, Patty, Elaine, Elise, Jon, Carshena, Lynnette, Curt, Marti, and many, many others. Neighbors and friends were incredibly supportive and tolerant, inviting the children to events, providing meals when disarray prevailed, intervening when it was evident I needed help, providing safe homes for Alec and coming to my aid no matter what time I might call. To name a few: JoAnn, John, Debbie, Laura, George, Judy, Eric, Ed, Roz, Tim, Diane, Vickie, Carolyn, Colleen, Marge, Michael, Carl, April, Bill, Richard, Nila, Betty, Luda and Stella. A few warrant special note such as Theresa who actually watched the children for five days in a hurricane, without electricity, while my professional obligations required me to be elsewhere; and Phebe and Jake who remained unfazed by any shenanigans that might take place during one of our visits. I'd like to also recognize some very important educators and professionals who went above and beyond to patiently and lovingly guide my children in learning academic basics and appropriate social interactions – Karen, Colleen, Bonnie, Eric, Ms. Weaver, Jennifer, Linda, Lindsey, Judy, Traci, Patsye, Marsha, Ms. Drain, and Mary. The staff at The Bridges will always be remembered for truly loving Alyona and tenderly supporting us during many trying times – Dr. Henderson, Heather, Jennifer and all of the nurses. Endurance accolades go to the sitters – Annie, Michelle, Rebecca, Talia, Melissa, Maleka, Rich – who withstood physical and emotional duress but always responded with kind, but firm, guidance. The patient, flexible and caring personal and professional support at work made it possible for services to be unaffected when those unexpected crisis calls occurred. Special thanks to Aleta, Julie, Judi, Marian, Rich, Terri, Jeff, Terri, Louise, Cathy, Jeff and Robert. And I would like to thank the quasi support group of mothers (especially Patty and Sherry) who adopted older children from Ukraine – the commiseration was healing. Adaptability was a welcomed trait of my monthly bridge group which frequently had to compensate for one less player when I was called away by a frantic, and often frightened, sitter. Some have already been mentioned in other capacities but I add to the list – Carolyn, Rhoda and Maureen. I will always be indebted to Ilona and Svetta who helped me literally start my family and welcomed us all with open, loving arms. I'm most appreciative to the police and EMTs who were called to our home on several occasions and responded with professionalism and wisdom. And finally, the many strangers who may have seen us struggling at an ice hockey game and got out of line to sit with us to help calm the storm; the baseball spectators/parents and players who wisely supported, rather than made fun of, the children's bizarre antics; the woman at a festival event who used humor to calm Alyona when I was obviously at my wit's end and the numerous grocery store patrons who, rather than criticize the loud and disruptive behavior, attempted to reassure me with a "My kids have their days, too." My sincerest apologies to the many persons whose names I have inadvertently failed to include – it is not meant as a slight but rather a reflection of my poor memory for the far too numerous-to-count people who, without hesitation, came to our aid making a happy ending possible. Thanks to all.

Foreword

Katharine C. Kersey, Ed.D.

I was flattered when my friend, Nancy Welch, invited me to write an introduction to her book, *Healing Emotional Wounds – A Story of Overcoming the Long Hard Road to Recovery from Abuse and Abandonment*, which tells about her adoption of two abused and neglected six-year old children from the Ukraine. When I read her story, I was taken back by the way she had handled this "adventure," which turned out to be much more than she ever bargained for.

My interest in this topic had heightened since I had been asked to serve on a dissertation committee for a student who has now graduated with her PhD from Duquesne University. I learned so much from working with her as she wrote on "The Lived Experience of Parenting a Child Adopted from an Institution in Eastern Europe." She had interviewed eleven parents who had experienced heart-wrenching episodes with their adopted children from Russia, the Ukraine and Siberia. She recounted many of their experiences and told the frustrations that they had encountered, such as their adopted children injuring their siblings, playing one parent against the other, lying and threatening to kill their parents and run away from home.

I thought I was prepared to know the kinds of challenges that Nancy would have experienced, but there was no way that I could have known what she was facing as she embarked on her journey.

Nancy chose to go through a private agency and made one trip to Ukraine to see the institutionalized children before she committed to adopt. Once she made up her mind, there was no turning back. Six months later, after being bombarded with paperwork and filling out documents in duplicates and triplicates – establishing her identity and testifying to her physical, mental and financial stability, she was ready to return to Ukraine to adopt two little children.

Strangely enough, a student who was working on her masters in public health heard about her intention and offered to go to the Ukraine and help her bring the children back to the States. What a blessing that turned out to be.

When it was time to choose her children, Nancy was drawn to Alec right away. He acted like a clown and it was obvious that he wanted to make others happy.

He was helpful and energetic and she felt happy just watching him. She named him Alec Edwin Welch before officially choosing him. Alyona was a different child. She had a stoic façade, a certain defiance about her and was described by the caretaker as "stubborn," "a good helper," and "very smart." Nancy had the strange feeling that she and this child were of the same spirit, that she knew this child and that she was "meant to be" Alyona Mae Welch.

More paper work, offers of bribes, and long periods of waiting followed, but finally Nancy emerged euphoric, clutching the final papers – realizing that at last she was approved for adoption by the Social Services Board (with the expectation that she would make an "appropriate donation" to the orphanage.)

Soon Nancy was on her way to an apartment owned by the woman with whom she had been staying – with her two six-year-old children. She was totally unprepared for what happened next. As soon as Alec and

Alyona realized that they were "free," all hell broke loose. They became wild: screaming, throwing toys, jumping on beds, pouring perfume, pushing buttons, throwing books, breaking glass, creating bedlam everywhere.

Nancy was at a real disadvantage – not speaking their language and knowing that they had no way to understand her. Nancy realized quickly that she was in no way prepared for her future with these children. This would be the greatest challenge of her life.

The student who had promised to accompany her on their trip to the States had arrived and was getting to know these children the hard way. They were not kind to her either and treated her with disrespect and scorn.

Therefore, it was with fear and trepidation that these two women set out for their long trip "home." Shortly after take-off, the children started. They refused to wear their seat belts, threw magazines, headphones and shoes. Grabbing books and toys, they escaped to empty seats across the aisle and ran to pull the lever that would open the cabin's big rear door. If they were held, the children screamed and pulled hair, and if they were not held, they ran wild: kicking people, suitcases and chairs. Other passengers were getting very annoyed, "Can't you control your kids?" "Give them to me and I'll get them to behave." "You have no business having kids if you can't handle them." "They need a good spanking –mother **and** children." "They should give medicine to the children to make them sleep." When they arrived at their layover in Amsterdam, the stewardess escorted them to the VIP lounge and said in a loud whisper that it was for "very irritating passengers."

On August 30, 1999, Nancy arrived home with her new life in front of her. She was relieved on the one hand to be among friends who spoke the same language, and she was confidant of her own parenting skills, but she also knew that the road to creating a loving, caring family would be difficult and challenging. In her heart she was convinced that parenting Alec and Alyona would be hard, but adopting them was the RIGHT thing to do. She said a silent prayer for wisdom, patience, compassion and humility. The rest of the book is a testament to the strength that it took for Nancy to achieve her dream. Thankfully, she had many natural resources upon which she could draw: self-confidence, a spirit of adventure, persistence, independence, resilience, the willingness to ask for help, and a trust in her own intuition to face the challenges which these children presented. She was determined to make every day a "new day," to learn from her mistakes and not to beat up on herself.

There were times when the children had uncontrollable rage – kicking dirt in Nancy's face, hitting her with their fists, biting her hands and spitting in her face. They pulled her hair, slugged for no reason, kicked her in the shins and had to be restrained and locked in their rooms.

Finally, with the help of a therapist, Nancy realized that a history of severe abuse had left deeply embedded scars on Alyona and she had to be admitted to a residential facility four and a half hours away. For the next 20 months, Nancy and Alec made trips every week to be with her. Sometimes they were only allowed to see her for a half hour because of unresolved behavior issues. Nancy made every trip a learning adventure and found countless resources nearby to enjoy and from which they could learn.

Even after she was discharged, Alyona continued to have repeated tirades at home, sometimes of such magnitude that Nancy had to call for police intervention. During the years that followed, Alyona continued to have tantrums where she destroyed furniture, walls, doors and lamps and even kicked and broke her mother's car windshield. After having charges pressed against her and facing probation and court appearances, she finally realized that she had lost belief in herself and eventually took control of her own life and behaviors.

This book, *Healing Emotional Wounds – A Story of Overcoming the Long Hard Road to Recovery from Abuse and Abandonment,* is an inspiration to anyone who reads it. The abuse that Nancy endured is unbelievable. It is even hard to read. Perhaps the children thought that Nancy would "give up on them," perhaps they were testing her – to see if she would send them back. But she did not weaken. It is a testament to Nancy's strength and determination, hard work and commitment that she never gave up hope and held onto her dream – knowing that they would eventually have to heal themselves. She was able to provide the environment conducive to their healing – where they would eventually be able to trust her love and settle into a gentle, comfortable bond of family.

Prologue

I wish I could say that I have always wanted to have children, that I had a burning desire to be a mother; it would be easier to explain why I adopted. But it would be a lie. Mind you, I always felt connected with children and have known since childhood that I wanted to be a pediatrician. While I was in high school, baby-sitting was almost my full-time job. I was able to communicate with kids of all ages. I was reliable, and parents readily trusted me to feed their children, bathe them, change their diapers, and put them to bed on time. As the oldest girl among five siblings, I had far more extensive experience caring for kids than most people my age.

I enjoyed the spontaneity and unpredictability of children, was enthralled with the magic of how they learned and grew. I found it fascinating that skills such as smiling, holding a spoon or cup, feeding themselves, talking, walking, riding a tricycle and reading seemed to happen in all of them at about the same age. I used to play a game with myself of guessing the age of a child according to his or her skills.

I loved children's sheer joy and excitement at so many simple pleasures —blowing bubbles, being pushed in a swing or being chased around the yard. They made me laugh. They challenged my creative spirit. They reminded me to enjoy life.

Yet I never imagined myself as a mother; a caretaker for others' children, yes, but not with children of my own. I wasn't consciously aware that I had any real adversity to the idea; I just didn't see myself as a mother.

Around 1995 or 1996 a friend, who is a therapist by profession, broached the subject of adoption. It seemed to just come out of the blue. "Nancy, you ought to consider adopting a child," she told me. "You'd be a good mother."

I was only slightly startled by the suggestion, as my friend was known to interject the unexpected into conversation. Besides, I was single, financially secure and in my early fifties, so perhaps it wasn't too bizarre an idea. Still.

"You're good with children, patient and laugh easily," my friend said. "You don't take yourself too seriously and don't mind being embarrassed. You're very good at encouraging and supporting people to feel good about themselves."

Still.

She delivered her coup de grace. "You could provide a good home and family to a child who might not otherwise have one. You could help a child grow and reach his fullest potential. You're an excellent caretaker and that's exactly what an adopted child, or any child, needs."

There it was, the caretaker word. She knew that would appeal to me. I grew up in a family that emphasized how important it is to help others, whether or not they're immediate kin. We very often had children or adults who, for whatever reason, stayed with us for a time. There were friends whose families were in conflict, friends experiencing financial problems, and all needed shelter and respite. Others were strangers who had met my parents through fortuitous encounters at work, or who'd been given Mom's name by someone. Mom had a sense about people troubled or needing assistance, and a heart that never turned them away.

Having been raised in this environment, it was a natural and easy transition to pursue a career in medicine. Being a physician, for me, was the epitome of service and caring for others. Pediatric residency was intellectually fulfilling but a painful, emotional roller-coaster. I seemed to be cursed with a black cloud; I drew a disproportionate amount of the rare and complex cases. The stress was overwhelming, so much so that I almost left pediatrics. But a wise and gentle professor steered me towards community health, building on the strong preventive ideology common in pediatrics. I've been very content as a public health director since 1976.

I once met a young man from Africa who was working at the hospital for the summer, as I was. He mentioned that he was sleeping in one of the offices and asked if I knew where he might find a room. I immediately gave him our address and invited him to stay with us. Not once did I think about calling my mother to confirm that it would be acceptable. He was welcomed with open arms. There was only one caveat: Mom was a lousy cook. Anyone staying at our house learned very quickly they had to feed himself.

As an adult, I have assumed Mom's legacy. It's not unusual for me to have friends or acquaintances stay at my home when they are experiencing difficult chapters in their lives. My former sister-in-law and her three children stayed at my home for almost two years. My youngest nephew was still in diapers. My brother and his wife were having a difficult time so I was glad to help. One summer I had five college boys stay at my home. The next summer I had five girls from England. I still correspond with the girls and, in fact, have visited them in Great Britain. Some people visit sick people in the hospital or take meals to shut-ins. I'm not very good at either. I welcome people into my home and family and provide a safe and, hopefully, healing environment.

The caretaker pitch clinched it. I decided to start the adoption process with an adoption agency. And thus begins my story. Through a series of providential experiences I was led to Ukraine and the adoption of two abused and neglected six-year old children. My family was created, and my resolve birthed to help these children heal.

The gift granted me was more than motherhood. It was the opportunity to transform pain and chaos into hope and beauty. Together, we have traveled a very rough road. Our pathway has been nothing like I learned in my medical training. There has been violence, mayhem and fear, as well as laughter, resiliency, humility and recovery. But my belief in my children and our ad-hoc little family has never waned. Just as heat transforms rough sand into smooth glass, so the sometimes hellish and always challenging process of building trust and love has fused three distinct and disparate lives into a single strong entity. Here's hoping this story provides inspiration and encouragement to others attempting something similar.

PART I

Adoption

Chapter 1

"It was the voices," the psychiatrist says. "They were telling Alyona to kill both you and her teacher."

The room is hot and stuffy. There are no windows and no pictures on yellowed walls long overdue for a paint job. The desk is bare. I try to focus on the psychiatrist's dark but kind eyes. She is looking right at me. Instead, I notice how well she is dressed and I admire her olive-toned skin and attractive Mediterranean features. Her face is a soft sculpture. This is not her office—she would have pictures. This is the room where they bring parents to give them bad news about their children. Alyona hearing voices telling her to kill me is bad news.

"We are adjusting medications to help stabilize her. But your daughter is a very sick little girl who will need extensive, long-term treatment," the psychiatrist continues. "She was severely traumatized at a very impressionable young age."

The words slowly penetrate my conscience. She's talking about my seven-year-old daughter, who was abandoned or lost and on the streets at age four.

Alyona only has fleeting memories of a mother, dad and one or two siblings. She has no reliable recall as to why she was by herself or what happened to her family. She remembers being hungry, very hungry. She remembers begging for food, and how good a hunk of bread tasted. Most of all she remembers being terribly afraid at night. She thinks she spent two nights in a tree; she had to stay awake to keep her grip on the branches and keep from falling. Nightfall brought scary creatures and bizarre sounds that she attributed to vicious animals or even more vicious people. Everything and everybody became more villainous when cloaked in shadows, when voices were distorted and faces covered. She has faint images of her mother reading to her, and the safe feeling of cuddling next to the woman, whom she remembers as pretty. She thinks she had a favorite toy, but doesn't remember what it was. She remembers the big boys on the street giving her food. That's about all.

I adopted her just fifteen months ago from Ukraine. Now she's had a meltdown at school, and requires an emergency hospital admission. The psychiatrist tells me that Patsye has recommended that I commit Alyona, and then adds: "I agree that she should be admitted to The Bridges."

My heart protests but my lips say, "I know."

⌒⌒

Stunned by what I knew were going to be challenging times ahead, I asked myself what made me think I was capable or skilled enough to adequately parent this child, to help her heal. Then I realized how my life had prepared me from childhood. The refrain "I'll find a way" has been my mantra all my life. I learned it from my mother. My parents were high school sweethearts, graduating during the Depression. My dad was valedictorian but unable to attend college because he didn't have the money. He never could quite focus on a single line of work, although his most consistent income came from owning a laundromat and driving a school bus. My mother, by her own admission, majored in boys and theater. She became a hairdresser. In reality, though, I believe she was a pseudo-therapist. She was blessed with phenomenal insights and wisdom and people in need were drawn to her like a magnet.

We had very little money for a family with five children, of whom I was the second overall and the oldest of three girls. Even though the cupboards might be bare, Mom always maintained a positive attitude. She would reassure us: "We'll find a way. God doesn't give you more than you can handle." We ate a lot of eggs, pancakes and peanut butter and jelly sandwiches. Boxed macaroni and cheese and canned spaghetti were staples. Babysitting gave me access to well-stocked kitchens and leftovers. None of us starved.

My parents built a wall to divide the downstairs into two living spaces so they could rent part of the house. As our family grew, and the renters were preparing to move, mom insisted that the wall be torn down so we would have more room, but dad refused. One day we arrived home from school to find mom standing on a stool hacking away at the wall with a hatchet. We were unnerved by the sight of our mother with an axe. We begged her to stop. She continued to chop at the wall, pulling out strips of splintered wood as they loosened. Without looking at us, she declared, "Your daddy's not going to take this down so I found a way to do it."

Between my junior and senior year of high school, our parents gave us the bad news that the road in front of their hair salon and laundromat was to be widened, eliminating the parking for customers. They were going to have to close their business and they had no other jobs.

"I can share my babysitting money," I offered.

"Don't worry," my mom answered. "We'll find a way."

One of mother's customers had a friend who had a friend who had vacationed at a resort on Lake Champlain in Vermont. The customer suggested that mom contact the resort and see if our family could get summer jobs. I never questioned why they didn't just look in the newspaper for job openings. The idea of traveling to Vermont, though, assumed the spirit of an adventure; we had never been there and travel to mountains more than 1,400 miles away seemed exotic and exciting. Dad got a job as night watchman, mom as a hairdresser, my brother as a bellhop, and I worked in children's recreation. My bellhop brother and I lived in the staff quarters; my parents and the other three children lived in a rented cabin in the lakeside woods. In one decisive move my parents had transformed what could have been a crisis into a rich and exhilarating sojourn of new sights and experiences. This trip wasn't just a matter of survival; it was vacation and exploration. They understood that they'd have to find jobs on our return, but they deferred the challenge. For the time being, they had found a way.

I learned to trust the refrain, "We'll find a way," as a promise. No matter the circumstance, my parents always kept us clothed, fed and sheltered. I learned to be adaptable and to believe that any problem could, and would, be solved. I learned to confront unexpected hurdles as challenges. I concealed my occasional uncertainty or fear into remote crevices of my thought, and instead focused on how to resolve the problem at hand.

When I was fourteen I got a job babysitting a family of three children. The family introduced me to Dale Carnegie's book, How to Win Friends and Influence People. When the parents would come home to have lunch with the children, I would sit on the front porch and digest Carnegie's words. From him I learned the value of sincerity and diplomacy. I might never have read the book were it not for the fact that I needed the job. I developed an unshakeable belief that solving problems with which I was confronted could bring important lessons, along with a sense of accomplishment and exciting new experiences.

My father introduced me to the joy of reading. Many nights, with a book and a large Hershey bar tucked under his arm, he would lead us upstairs to cuddle next to him while he read to us and, of course, to share the candy. I loved the menagerie of Mother Goose tales, the stories of Raggedy Ann and Andy, Mickey Mouse, Sky King, Lassie and one, that even to this day, I can hear again and again—Pinocchio. I was enamored with the written word and how it could make me laugh, root for characters, dance, or be willing to brave the unknown.

By sixth grade I had read all the biographies in our school library, so the principal borrowed books from other schools. My favorites were about Franklin and Eleanor Roosevelt, Helen Keller, Joan of Arc, Florence Nightingale and Albert Schweitzer. They were smart, engaged in life and champions of the underdog.

At dinner, Mom and Dad recited poems or excerpts from books. I would sit in awe each time they delivered a passage from "Annabelle Lee," "O Captain! My Captain!" or, my favorite, James Leigh Hunt's "Abou Ben Adhem." When Mom came to the part of the poem that goes, "I pray thee, then; write me as one who loves his fellow men," my heart would leap and shout, "Yes, Yes!"

As the oldest girl I often helped my mother with the younger children. I learned at a very young age how to prepare a croup tent over my brother's crib and found that his symptoms would ease if I sat with him in a steamy bathroom. I learned that by applying cool washcloths to my sister's neck and face I could sometimes reduce her fever enough that she wouldn't have a seizure. I became an expert at mixing the evaporated milk, water and Karo syrup in the proper proportion for the baby.

When my mother had to call the pediatrician in the middle of the night about one of the younger children, she would often delegate describing the symptoms to me. If we had to go to the emergency room, I would hold my brother or sister while the doctor conducted the examination. The doctor would refer to me as "Little Mother," and I'd beam with pride.

At times, though, being a "Little Mother" was a curse. It meant that many times I was "in charge" or responsible for my younger siblings. I took that charge seriously; I'm sure that what I saw as responsible shepherding looked bossy to everyone else.

It came as no surprise to my mother when, at ten years of age, I announced to her that I wanted to be a doctor, and a pediatrician, in particular. I wanted to take care of children and make them well. She smiled and told me, "You'll make a good one. You'll find a way."

The unspoken understanding in her response was that my parents could not help any of us to pay for college because they didn't have the money. We would have to manage on our own. When I went to Lynchburg College I worked forty hours a week around my classes, divided between shifts as an aide in the emergency room and a lab assistant, striving to cram my hours in from Friday afternoon to Sunday night. It was tiring but exciting. The doctors seemed excited by my questions and I was elated at all I was learning and seeing. In the summer I added more hours as secretary and switchboard operator so that I worked ninety to 110 hours per week. I had a goal in sight. I vigorously and compulsively worked towards that goal. I felt mature and responsible.

In November of my senior year I interviewed at medical schools. While at Duke University one of the faculty members asked me, "If we accept you, how will you pay for it?"

The irony of the question was that at the time I was in a quandary because after having paid the tuition for my final semester of college I had no money left to pay for room and board, and was scrambling to find a place where I could stay for free. A French professor would eventually agree to have me; at three in the morning two friends and I would "borrow" an unused bed from the dormitory and put it in the professor's emptied pantry. I had to stand sideways to dress, but the price was right.

My response to the Duke interviewer was immediate and simple: "You accept me and I'll find a way."

Duke accepted me.

Now, years later, I face my hardest demand to find a way. "You'll want to visit her as often as possible," the psychiatrist says.

I'm facing a concerned professional, but I see the image of Alyona in her pixie haircut. I form a reply within my head, but the words never leave my mouth: "I'm not a quitter. I'm a hard worker. Long odds don't deter me." And: "I love you, Alyona. I promise, little girl, I'll find a way."

Chapter 2

I didn't expect the guns. The vehicles sitting on the cracked and crumbling runway were military-issue, bristling with mounted guns. Soldiers were stationed near the gate, studying the plane and passengers as we stepped down the stairs, their rifles slung over shoulders or at post arms. They barked orders in no-nonsense Russian. Neither my sister, Robbie, nor I spoke the language, but their tone was easy to read. We got in line with other passengers. A soldier yelled at us and waved the barrel of his rifle towards another line. We were quick to obey. We heard the word "passport," and had ours ready when we reached the desk. The clerk studied our documents and faces before letting us pass. I'm a guest here. I've done nothing wrong. Still, I felt guilty of something.

I'd done my homework and knew that Odessa, with a population of over one million, was the fourth-largest city in Ukraine. It had been a popular tourist destination with its many spas and resorts, at least before the collapse of Communism in 1991 and the country's independence. But there was no mention of the military in the articles I read to prepare for this trip in January 1999. I did not expect the guns.

⌒

It seems like an eternity, yet it's been less than two weeks since Vinny knocked on my door on a cold Saturday morning. When we had talked by phone he had spoken passionately about the Ukrainian orphanages his organization supported, his words coming in such a lively, rapid-fire stream that it was difficult to interject any questions. He raved about how his organization had repaired roofs, painted building interiors, supplied teaching materials and instituted a job-training program. His goal was not to sell his organization, but to sell the value of the children in the orphanages. They were worth every penny, every second and every exhausting bit of labor put into providing them a better place to live and a hope for their future, he gushed. He believed these children could be saved and that we had an obligation and responsibility to attempt their rescue. He was committed to improving their lives. He had been referred to me by an adoption agency where I had previously been registered.

In fact, he had contacted me several weeks before about a 12-year-old girl from Nicaragua whom his organization had brought to the States for medical care and for whom he had hoped to find an adoptive home before she had to return. As it happened, he'd phoned the agency where my name was on record. They informed him that they only handled newborns and infants, but, that night the director woke several times thinking of me. The next morning she'd called Vinny. "Call Nancy," she'd told him. "I'm not sure she was primarily interested in an infant. An older child may work out even better."

She must have perceived my discomfort during the required group meetings of potential adopting parents. I had felt totally out of place. I was like a robot at a sensitivity retreat. Women revealed heart-wrenching stories of how they had always wanted to be a mother and had tried for many years, unsuccessfully, to get pregnant. They spoke of their childhood fantasies, their dolls, and how inadequate they felt without children. Tears flowed freely. The other women in the room nodded in accord.

I was concerned what I would say when it was my turn. I never liked playing with dolls or having tea parties as a kid. I preferred playing catch, climbing trees, playing kickball, riding my bike, reading, imagining myself a cowgirl in the Wild West and, of course, making people feel better with the tools in my play-doctor bag. My parents gave me a doll once and I promptly gave it back to them with the stern response, "I don't like dolls." They never gave me another.

"Nancy, it's your turn."

I slumped a bit in my seat. "I think I would make a good mother and provide a nurturing home environment where a child could thrive and feel good about himself," I offered. There. Concise and to the point.

The other women in the group eyed me expectantly. I didn't have more to say. I managed a weak smile, and the woman to my left mercifully began her story: "I have had three miscarriages and I'm afraid to get pregnant again." The Director had grasped the reasons for my discomfort better than I.

So, at her referral, I spent time with Vinny and the young girl. I went with her to her doctor's appointments and ate lunch with her several times. She was already enamored with many Western amenities. She insisted on watching television constantly and was an expert with a remote control. She craved being the center of attention and was attuned to the latest fashions. I was unable to connect with her. I felt that, in her mind, it was my role to compensate her for all the wrongs she had experienced in her young life. This was not how I wanted to start my family. I halted the proceedings.

Now Vinny and I sat in my kitchen looking at pictures of younger children in orphanages in Ukraine. Most had blond hair and blue eyes, but there was no sparkle to their expressions; their smiles seemed exaggerated and contrived. Vinny had a story about each child: She has a beautiful voice and loves to sing. He studies hard in school. She helps take care of the younger children. She always says, "Thank you." He never gets in trouble.

He knew the pictures had captured my interest and, like a car salesman eager to close on the purchase, he excitedly interjected: "I'm leaving in two days and will be there for two weeks. It would be nice if you could come visit so I can show you the children. But I'll have to know by tomorrow."

Half-chuckling, I said I'd let him know. I was chuckling because right at that moment in my purse I had my passport and airline ticket in preparation for an upcoming trip to Scotland with my sister and brother-in-law. It was incredible serendipity. Several months before, on a whim, I had called my sister in Florida and casually asked, "What do you think about you, your husband and me taking a vacation to Scotland?" Robbie, always eager for travel and adventure, had quickly said, "Yes." The dates for our trip fell within the two weeks Vinny suggested I visit. It did not take long to convince Robbie to rearrange a schedule for the side-trip to Ukraine.

"I'm sorry, Ma'am, but all the flights to Chicago have been canceled due to a blizzard." Thinking I had heard her wrong I asked the ticket agent to repeat what she'd said. Her words were the same; I couldn't get to Chicago where I was to join Robbie for the flight to Europe. Robbie had already boarded in Florida and was unreachable. On the drive to the airport, I had reveled in the beauty of the snow-covered branches and the excitement of those few eager children who defied the usual Saturday sleep-in to venture outdoors in pre-dawn darkness to laugh and roll in the snow. I had smiled with delight, oblivious to the weather's impact on air travel. Now I stood at the counter with a line of people behind me and the sandy-blond, middle-aged woman behind the counter staring at me. The snow had lost its magic.

The ticket agent patiently inquired: "Is it more important that you meet with your sister here in the States or assume that you both will make it to Odessa?" Aware of my quandary, she deftly posed the key question that was both caring, yet also effective in moving me out of the line. "Get me to Odessa," I said.

A few hours and two plane transfers later I was headed over the ocean to Frankfurt, Germany. The mystery novel I'd packed, although steeped in unpredictable intrigue, was unable to keep my attention. I clung to the long, blue down coat I had brought for Robbie, wondering if it was snowy and cold wherever she had to change planes. Outside was total blackness. It has always amazed me how the stars are so bright and sparkling when viewed from the ground and yet they become lost in the darkness as you fly closer to them. I gazed at nothing and yet at everything. I spoke to no one yet never felt alone. I dozed and when I woke we were coming into Frankfurt.

I exited the plane to an airport under major construction. My high school German long forgotten, I could understand only fragments of my surroundings; my vocabulary did not include "detour" or "Gate x has been changed to Gate y," and I got "right" and "left" backwards—a handicap, in that my departure gate was in a different and distant terminal. After walking past the same snack bar about five times I finally arrived at my gate. I was too tired to read but too much of a people watcher to sleep. I tried to imagine the topic of conversation of an animated young couple, the title of the book being read by an elderly, gray-haired woman and the rules of the board game being played by two young children. The laughter of two young women sounded the same in German as in English. I waited patiently for the flight to be announced.

"Nancy, I'm so glad to see you."

Robbie strode into the waiting area her usual smiling and bubbly self. She was the petite member of the family, with blond, short-cropped hair that was always in place. No matter the occasion, her make-up was subtle but perfect. Her everyday effervescence spoke to the Miss Congeniality award she'd won while competing in a beauty pageant years before. Her casual entry gave an air that we were merely meeting for lunch. She quickly donned the promised winter coat. We chatted about the weather, the flights, the people, and the food. In contrast to me, Robbie can always find a subject to discuss.

When we arrived at Odessa, the airport "terminal" was a small building with paint peeling from its walls. It felt dim and dingy. Stern-faced soldiers, clutching rifles close to their side, directed traffic along a narrow corridor. The baggage claim was a mere space on the floor where the attendants dumped the luggage. The walk from the gate to the lobby was shorter than the walk from my Virginia living room to my bedroom. Passengers crowded through the narrow entranceway. We entered the lobby to the gleeful shouts of "Nancy, over here." I looked towards the voice and saw a tall, black-haired woman with sharp cheekbones. She glowed with excitement and waved me over. Her other hand held two red roses. I had no idea who she was, but I sure was glad to see her.

She quickly glided towards us, smoothly parting the crowd. Even the gun-toting soldiers casually moved out of her way at her bidding. When she reached us she gave us hugs and kisses on each cheek. She was Luda, she announced in perfect English, and Vinny had sent her. At her side was Igor, our driver, a short, soft-spoken man whose broad smile revealed white, well cared-for teeth and who let Luda do all the talking while he listened intently, looking each of us in the eye when we spoke. Their apparent jubilation at my arrival made my lost suitcase seem trivial. It was easy to be swept up in their excitement.

Before leaving the airport I told Luda I needed to use the restroom. She immediately opened her purse and handed me a wad of toilet paper, "Here, use this. It's softer and there's probably not any in the bathroom anyway."

Astounded, I wanted to say, "But it's 1999 and this is a huge city," but only nodded my thanks. Luda, it seemed, was a smart, savvy woman who'd learned to adapt to the time warp that grips much of the former Soviet Union. She directed me down a short hallway and to a battered door. As soon as I opened it I had to take a step back—the room within reeked; its concrete floor was filthy with scattered dirt and dust-balls and pocked with holes. There had been an attempt to paint the walls, but it had happened long before. Inch-long brown bugs with large wings folded on their backs crawled about. A single bare bulb dangled from the ceiling, casting a dim glow. To one side were two ancient porcelain sinks, deeply scratched, a steady column of water leaking from one faucet. On the far wall was an elevated platform supporting two stalls. The doors were louvered. Even the rustic Girl Scout camp I attended in the fifties had offered more privacy.

As the women left the stalls I thought, "How rude, they are not flushing the toilet." I glanced in a vacated stall. There was another small concrete platform with a big hole in the middle through which I could see the raw sewage underneath. There was no toilet seat. The base platform had worn areas, shaped like shoes, on either side of the hole.

Although I had served in the Army Reserve for almost twenty years and had done tours in remote places like the jungles of Panama and the Mojave Desert I had never seen anything like this. It was difficult to reconcile "fourth-largest city" and "major tourist destination" with the structure before me.

Once inside the car, Luda boasted about Odessa. She talked of its rich orthodox history and architecture, its plentiful supply of flowers, its many spas. With great sadness in her voice, she also spoke of its poverty, joblessness, drug trade and abandoned children. She had grown up in Odessa and had beautiful memories of the place. Only since independence had the country struggled. She longed for a return to good times, and even more, children spared the heartbreak of disease, poverty or prostitution by being adopted and given another chance.

Now came the questions: "Will you adopt a child?" she asked me. "What ages in the orphanage do you want us to see first?"

"I'm not sure if I'm going to adopt or not," I told her. "I wanted to first visit the country and see some of the children and the orphanages." I added: "I'm most interested in children from two years up to ten."

I had settled on that age when I'd actually felt relieved that I wasn't selected by any birth mother through the agency, to adopt a newborn. Rather than being disappointed or insulted, I had whispered a thank you. I had not been honest with myself: I'd blindly followed a route that I perceived was expected of me, namely, that women naturally want babies and enjoy playing with infants. I didn't; and I needed to give myself permission to admit, without shame, my preference. Beyond the physical examination of an infant, I really didn't know what to do with a baby. I'm not the cooing type. I can only marvel at the fingers, toes, nose, ears and focus of the eyes but so many times. I didn't really see myself in a rocking chair feeding a baby, or carefully bathing this fragile being. And since I'm innately a very private person, I most assuredly couldn't imagine receiving well-meaning attention and admiration of the baby by strangers in grocery stores and on walks around the lake. Perhaps I feared that having a baby would send a message, or expose an emotion, that I wanted to be a mother. Being a strong thinker who prefers to mask my feelings in logic, reasoning, and words, I didn't want to risk such discomfort.

I like being able to communicate with children. I'm enthralled with their perceptions and responses to the world around them. I'm fascinated with their exploration of every little thing—examining and following a bug, creating sounds with pans, spoons, boxes, their spontaneous laughter at a funny hat, their delight at discovering that with the press of a button they can make a remote-control car move or a radio talk. Witnessing a child's discovery renews the discovery for me, reopens my eyes to the invigorating world around us. It reminds me to be grateful, and to tend to life with gentleness and respect. As Wordsworth said, "The child is father of the man." That is truly the case: Although life may at times seem a mystery, I can never doubt its significance when I permit myself to see it through the eyes of a child.

We drove to the hotel. It was a beautiful, ornately designed building over a century old. The lobby's carpet depicted Russian dancers in rich colors, and beautiful carved statues were all about. It was a building with a history of grand times and balls and visits by famous people. It was a building standing tall amidst struggle and poverty. It was a building that insisted that it not be overlooked.

The day after our arrival was windy and bitingly cold. Bundled in our long coats, we arrived at an orphanage for children four to six years old, just as they were coming outdoors for "exercise." It took the form of a march around the playground, their handlers taking pains to keep them in step and in line. They looked like a caterpillar with intermittent bulging, round sections, these being the children cocooned in multiple layers for warmth. You could hardly tell the boys from girls except for those few children who lacked hats or earmuffs. None of their coats were equal to the weather, so they'd been layered into a snowman-like roundness.

The yard was without grass, swing set, or toys. When the marching stopped, many of the kids stood expressionless, gazing at nothing. A few of the boys played running games. Many children swarmed us with outreached hands shouting, "mama, mama." As a single woman in her mid-fifties I felt a bit odd being called "mama." But then, they called even the male driver "mama."

En route to the orphanage for children over ten years old, I leaned my head on the glass and stared out the window trying to understand the city around me. It seemed as if I had a front-row seat for an interactive production of "Our Town." Flower shops abounded. The women, Luda among them, wore short skirts, mostly black, stiletto heels and thick make-up. I shivered at the thought of walking in the twenty-degree cold so barely attired.

The men wore suits and walked with purpose. How slovenly Robbie and I must have appeared in our typical American blue jeans, sweaters and sneakers.

The second orphanage housed close to three hundred children. Many of them ran freely on the grounds at our arrival and several dashed to Robbie and me. "Take me to America," they shouted. "I am good." Some espoused their skills: "I clean." "I smart." They pointed at us and displayed broad smiles, showing many rotten teeth. They conferred with each other. I felt like I had just stumbled into a community auction; they had placed themselves on the auction block and displayed their wares, hoping I would choose them. Some seemed able to penetrate my thoughts—they changed their behaviors and claims to match what they thought I wanted.

That evening Robbie and I purchased the most expensive tickets ($5.25 each) for the Tchaikovsky opera, "Swan Lake," which was playing at The Odessa Opera and Ballet Theater. The hotel arranged transportation in a private car. Twilight gave a magical ambience to a city that seemed to be just awakening. There was high energy in the air: Well-dressed couples strolled along tree-lined boulevards, cuddling close against the biting chill of the night. Women wore long fur coats over sequined, short skirts, their high heels clicking on the sidewalks. And dirty-faced children pulled winter ski caps snug around their faces and wrapped torn winter coats tightly around their bodies. Where would they sleep tonight and how would they stay warm? Street-lights illuminated some characters while others scurried in the darkness, only to emerge as main characters on the next block.

Elegant Mediterranean, French, Orthodox Russian and Art Nouveau architecture formed the backdrop for exquisitely attired walkers, overflowing trash cans and scruffy bearded men clutching open bottles in brown paper bags. High culture thrived amidst poverty and cheap amusements. I could appreciate the words of the Russian poet, Alexander Pushkin, referring to Odessa: "It was a city where you can smell Europe; French is spoken; and there are European papers and magazines to read."

A major seaport located on the Black Sea, this city of over one hundred ethnicities attributes its European style to the Duke de Richelieu. In 1803 Tsar Alexander I gave Richelieu the governorship of Odessa in gratitude for his leadership of the Russians against the Turks at Ismail. The young Frenchman slashed trade duties and officially dedicated one-fifth of the port's income to beautifying the city. Though Odessa still boasted the diverse and gilded architecture of Richelieu's Age, as well as the European culture he promoted, I wondered whether he could have foreseen the filth and degradation that would befall his beloved city.

Climbing out of the car and looking up at the Opera House's facade, it seemed obvious that the building was intended as a municipal focal point. The architecture was extravagantly ornate, with intricate stone details around every window and huge doorway, and sculptures representing characters of ancient Greek mythology. A beautiful Byzantine dome dominated the building's roof and occupied a prominent place in Odessa's skyline.

The interior was no less magnificent; over twenty-two pounds of gold of the highest standard was used in its renovation in 1967. The ceilings were sheathed in mosaics glinting with the metal. We trod marble floors and elegant rugs, among well-preserved antiques sprinkled about the lobby. Winding, marble staircases conjured images of long-past formal affairs.

The graceful, yet powerful, ballet was a good match for such surroundings. The music was like a warm cocoon protecting us from the stench and poverty outside, a world within a world.

The next day, Igor and Luda drove us to a restaurant where we were introduced to Ilona, a soft-spoken, slight young woman. Over a lunch typically abundant with potatoes, we talked about her experiences in negotiating private adoptions as an advocate, advisor, translator, and facilitator for would-be parents, primarily foreigners. She was blunt about her frustrations with the Ukrainian government and the childcare agencies, which were expert at creating unnecessary delays, demands and reviews—unless, that is, you were willing to pay thousands of dollars in bribes. She refused to work with anyone who agreed to such terms, she said, and condemned her colleagues who encouraged clients to do so to expedite the adoption process. I instantly trusted her.

"Have you decided to adopt?" She spoke in perfect English and focused her dark eyes on me. Although her heart clearly pained for the thousands of orphaned children she saw in the course of her work, she made no effort to persuade me to adopt.

"I'm still not sure," I told her. "If I adopt," I added, "I want a boy and a girl and I want to adopt them at the same time."

"I know how hard it can be for adopted children to overcome their past and become part of a family," Robbie said. "I adopted three at once from Social Services. They are still struggling. Nancy would be a good mother, though, and having seen my children she's not blind to the challenges."

"What are your concerns?" Ilona gently asked.

"How do you communicate with scared little children when you can't even speak their language?" I asked. "How do you ease their fears? Why would they trust me, a stranger? How do I switch from professional to mother? Do they even know about mothers and family?" I wasn't concerned about my ability to be a mother, I realized. I was concerned about teaching them to be a family, about helping them to thrive, and to truly escape desperate pasts. If I adopted, I was in it for the long haul, no pulling out. So how did I even choose the right children? I didn't want someone else to select them; it was important that I choose them and that they know for their entire lives that they were chosen.

"There are no guarantees, Nancy," both Ilona and Robbie said in unison.

"You need to decide if it is the right thing for you to do," Ilona added. "You will always have questions. But does it feel right?"

She spoke of the intensive work that would need to occur if I wanted to adopt. She was matter-of-fact about the many obstacles ahead. I identified with her logical and forthright approach. I had no illusions of a Disney family. In fact, I did best when the road was rocky: I knew, at such times, that I was making a difference. I realize that it might seem odd to some people, but even when purchasing rental properties I prefer those that require more work, time and engagement; I like being in the trenches and getting dirty, the awe and amazement of beauty emerging from shambles. I like believing in the future and potential of things or persons shunned or forsaken by others. I like finding the blossom hidden in the unsearched crevice that flourishes when exposed to the light. I don't like "easy." I know with complete confidence these truths about myself.

"Yes," I told Ilona, "I want to work with you to adopt a boy and a girl."

I had made the decision. In my mind, it was now engraved in stone. I'd stick with my commitments. It felt right. Like coming in from a snowstorm to sit in front of a roaring fire and sip a cup of hot chocolate—it felt warm and comfortable. I wanted to birth my family in Odessa, Ukraine.

Chapter 3

During nine months of pregnancy, a mother's waistline grows substantially. My "pregnancy," until my return to Ukraine six months later to adopt, resulted in an astronomical growth in paperwork. There were documents in duplicates and triplicates to complete, notarizations for Virginia, the United States Secretary of State and the Ukrainian embassy. I prepared documents establishing my identity and intent, confirmation of my physical, mental and financial stability, and signed some forms without ever fully comprehending their purpose.

It was easy, in the midst of this impersonal, bureaucratic process, to forget the faces, the eyes and the pleadings. Instead, I withdrew to a robot state, shuffling papers, reacting to requests, filling in blanks. I was ruled by deadlines and for the demanded data. No real sense of motherhood drove me onward. Yet I had a compelling belief that I was following a prescribed script, a mission. I was being obedient to a pathway established long before, and for which I, unknowingly, had been preparing all my life.

While a third-year medical student I had a similar experience. The school announced a highly competitive research scholarship and was seeking applications. I paid little attention, as I did not consider myself to be an academic-or research-oriented student. I preferred interactions with patients and clinical problem-solving. One night I had a very detailed dream that explicitly outlined the goals, objectives and methodologies for a research project related to prenatal education and birth outcomes. It entailed comparing study results in England and Sweden. I rarely remember dreams, so I saw in the vividness of this one a message. At three in the morning I rose from bed and began writing the proposal revealed in my dream. Later that day I obtained an application form and sought out hospitals in two countries where I could conduct the project. I intensely researched the topic. I was driven to submit a thorough, professional and compelling paper. Without a lick of experience in clinical research, or a previous desire to enter that field, I won the competition. It paid for me to conduct the research in London and Uppsala, Sweden, and the paper it enabled me to produce won a good deal of recognition.

Although I am very strongly oriented towards logical and scientific reasoning and thinking, I don't see it as contradictory to also be receptive to these inexplicable inner callings. I'm a woman of strong faith, evidenced more by how I live my life than any words or proclamations I might offer. I'm content just accepting some things without demands for proof. I also am comfortable with a diversity of beliefs. I find my life has been enriched by making room for both a scientific and a spiritual life. So I had no hesitation about avidly pursuing the adoption. I knew it was what I was meant to do.

⌒⌒

Oftentimes the silence of the newborns would haunt me, re-stoking my resolve. During our visit, Robbie and I had looked in on Odessa's Childrens Hospital, hoping to find it a more upbeat place than in the orphanage. Even if the abandoned children were neglected, we figured, surely the sick would receive decent care.

That's not what we found. There was no grass in the hospital's yard, no colorful pictures on the walls. The paint was peeling. Light bulbs had burned out. The elevator was not working, and the staff informed us that there was no money to fix it. Children had to be carried several floors for x-rays or diagnostic procedures, limited though they were.

Some meals were prepared on the floors, but most food, medications and clean sheets had to be brought in by the patients' families. Formula was supplied by the hospital, but in miserly dribs and drabs.

Half of the infants were HIV-positive. They received no medication and minimal attention—a diaper change a couple times a day and an occasional bottle left on their blankets. But the most distressing and eerie aspect of our visit was the absence of crying. The infants gazed blankly at their surroundings. Accustomed to wet and soiled diapers, they'd already learned that it was useless to cry for attention. Hours passed between feedings, yet they didn't cry. Their eyes were wide and sleepless; their bodies alert and unable to soften even when held gently and close to a beating heart. Most had been abandoned at birth. Their parents could not be found. And so they waited. They waited for lost parents. They waited for a home. They waited for love. Or they waited for death.

We visited the intensive care unit on one of the upper floors. Two doctors and a nurse were busily trying to insert an umbilical catheter in a sick newborn. Lacking a surgical lamp, they were performing the procedure by a large open window. They were gloveless. This would justify a malpractice suit anywhere in the West.

The neonatologist was bright and apologetic for what she knew to be the poor quality of care. She and her staff had no money for gloves, and often simply washed them between patients. They had no way to sterilize the areas in which they worked. Their respirators were a generation or more old, antiques by general medical standards.

Although Odessa was a big city, the hospital practiced medicine suited to a third-world country. The doctor had excellent training and was board-certified. As she spoke, her dark hazel eyes filled with tears. The best Robbie and I could do was to thank her for trying her best under the worst of circumstances. How difficult it must be to have the knowledge and skills to heal the sick, and yet be unable to do so because your government doesn't have the money to provide even remotely modern supplies, equipment or medicines. I know from experience how wrenching it is to tell parents that their child has died; but how much worse it must be when you know that elsewhere you might have saved him. Each time I remembered what I'd seen, my fortitude strengthened and I pressed on with the paperwork.

My sense that my path to adoption had been pre-ordained was sharpened about ten days before my scheduled return to Ukraine. As commonly occurs, a Masters in Public Health student, Laura, was doing an elective at our health department. I first met her at a meeting, at the close of which a nurse mentioned my upcoming trip and my intention to return with two children. "What an adventure," Laura said. "I've never even been west of the Mississippi."

Half joking, but only half, I replied, "So why don't you come along?"

"You know what? You can't bring two children back by yourself," she said. "I'll talk with my husband and come join you for the last two weeks so I can help you." The words rolled out of her mouth as if she had no control over what she was saying.

I later learned that Laura felt an immediate sense of panic, thinking: What have I done? How will I miss classes? How will I pay for this?

But at the time, she betrayed none of this, and I was speechless at so gracious an offer from a stranger. I knew she was right, of course—I couldn't bring two children back by myself. It seemed a moment of providence; I didn't question it.

"I'll pay for everything," I told her. "And maybe we can talk with the school and you can write a paper on your observations of public health in a foreign country." It must have seemed I'd read her mind.

And what followed, in retrospect, was almost crazily easy. Her husband was supportive. The school said yes to the paper idea. I helped her get a passport and schedule a flight to Ukraine. We were going. I was ready. All was in place.

Sleep was elusive. The cabin was dark save for a few scattered reading lights. The plane was full. In the silence I heard an occasional snore, the shift of a body, or a page turned. What prompted so many people to travel to Kiev, or anywhere else in Ukraine? I imagined some were on business trips involving complex international deals, or were natives headed home. I peered at the few I could make out in the gloom.

No one spoke, not even the attendants. The whir of the engine was rhythmic, hypnotizing. I felt almost detached from my physical being. I've never parachuted, but I imagine I felt something like one feels just before that leap from the plane into the wide open expanse of the sky—anticipation, trepidation, excitement, self-doubt, wishing it was over but not wanting to miss the exhilaration of the wind and the free-fall.

Suddenly, the lights came up. Over the cabin's speakers came the captain's voice: "Prepare your seatbacks for landing."

On my second arrival the military presence was not as shocking, but traveling alone made the language barrier all the more stark. With a sudden jolt, I comprehended that I was single, in a foreign land, and totally at the mercy of strangers to not only interpret but literally walk me through the maze of adoption. More frightening than the unfamiliar country and language was this surrender of my independence.

Svetlana was a tall, striking woman. Her erect posture suggested confidence and formality. Her dark black hair was shoulder-length, her skin smooth. She wore no makeup; here was a disciplined woman of no pretense. She held up a sign with my name on it. I waved and she walked with a quick, march-like stride towards me. Her English was not as sharp as Ilona's; she was curt in navigating me towards the car.

We rode to the oldest part of the city through narrow streets swirling with litter. Svetlana had made arrangements for me to stay at a hotel maintained by the International Baptist Church. Thankfully, she and the driver helped me lug my suitcases up the stairs, elevators being a luxury reserved for grander places. As we opened the door to my room, I was shocked by the oppressive heat, which made it almost difficult to breathe. Svetlana brushed the curtains aside and opened the single, screenless window. "It'll cool down in a little bit," she offered.

The absence of the smallest draft made me doubt that. Temperature aside, the room was simple but clean, with an old wooden dresser, a chair, and room to hang my clothes.

"Don't eat at the restaurants," Svetlana said on leaving, "because we've had problems with food diseases." So ended my reintroduction to Ukraine. Thankfully, I had packed many packages of Nabs, granola bars and nuts.

⌒

Kiev's morning sun forgoes subtlety and skips any gentle tap on the window pane. Rather, it arrives on the gallop; by five the room was awash in bright light.

I tore open a package of Nabs and another of trail mix, already longing for an IHOP or Cracker Barrel. I planned to ease into the day with a few minutes of reading. When sweat trickled down my face and onto the book, I decided it was time to explore.

Being careful to memorize street names and the turns I made, I meandered through the city, venturing into any lane that looked inviting. Out of curiosity I stepped into a large market. The interior was hot, the air still, and a pungent stink pervaded the space. At tables scattered throughout, vendors, with gloveless and bloody hands, proudly displayed the exceptional quality of chicken feet, wattles, combs and beaks; pig's feet; cow's tongue and heart; intestines; spinal columns; and slabs of bloody red muscle. None was on ice.

As one might gently squeeze a tomato to test for ripeness, customers stroked the inside of intestines, felt the firmness of liver and checked for spots along the spinal columns. After indicating their choice, the vendor would scoop up the meat with hands already bloodied from previous transactions and place it in a plastic bag. Blood dripping from the bag, the customer would trek through puddles of blood leaving red footprints. I felt I could almost see *E. coli* and *Salmonella*.

That afternoon Svetlana took me on a walking tour of Kiev, including the neighborhood in which she had grown up. It was a much prettier side of the city. The homes were freshly painted in cheerful peach, blue and yellow. Small yards with well-manicured shrubs and gardens peaked from among the houses, and well-dressed children walked the sidewalks, laughing easily. This Kiev seemed nothing like the city I'd explored in the morning.

But it was not Svetlana's Kiev: She showed me where her house had stood before it was torn down to make way for the city's upwardly mobile. She spoke fondly of roller-skating down the neighborhood's steep hill and of a carefree life; her reminiscence wasn't one of lost childhood so much as lost security, lost confidence. She felt lucky to have full time-work in a government office and to supplement her income by helping people with adoptions; she knew women who once had fine jobs teaching or in administration, but who now struggled to feed their children. Compared to them she was a success.

Back in my room, a cool breeze wafted through the open window. I could hear men and women gathered on the street, enjoying conversation in the pleasant summer evening. Only a rare car sped down the street. Sleep came effortlessly.

My dreamy state was rudely shaken at three AM by hostile shouts below my window. I heard what sounded like someone kicking a trash can, and voices began rising toward a peak at the exact moment that a projectile came sailing through my window and landed with a thud on the dresser. I stopped breathing and stared blindly into the darkness.

What had just happened? Who were these people? What had they thrown and why? Should I try to find it? Was it dangerous? Should I close the window? What would they do if they saw me at the window? Fearful paralysis, rather than curiosity, won out. I lay motionless.

Now came loud screaming in the hall and strong thumping on the door to my room. I realized with a twinge of panic that whoever had been outside a moment before could freely enter the hotel unchecked by security. I focused on the door. Had I remembered to lock it? I got my answer: someone pulled, turned and tugged at the doorknob. Maybe, I thought, putting the best possible spin on the situation, there's a fire, and these people, these noisy strangers, are merely alerting me to that fact. I listened intently to determine if there were crowds exiting the building or gathering on the street. I heard none. No police sirens either. I waited, my heart pounding. Eventually, my would-be visitors wandered off.

Silence returned; after awhile, so did my heartbeat's normal rhythm. When I woke early to almost ebullient sunshine, I was surprised to see, sitting on my dresser, as if part of the room's décor, a large, green granny smith apple.

Later that morning, Svetlana arrived to accompany me to the government offices where I'd obtain the authenticated documents required for adoption. We rode the bus to Kiev's government complex. In 1934, when the capital of the Ukrainian Soviet Republic was moved there from Kharkov, it was quickly evident that the city lacked the buildings and infrastructure it would need to accommodate the influx of officials and politicians; massive construction followed. All of the new government buildings were classical revival, busy with columns and pediments, wide steps, and massive in size. Masonry had been used extensively to reduce the reliance on rationed goods, such as steel. Much of this effort was wasted: Central Kiev had been destroyed in World War I when the Red Army destroyed the city to deny it to the Germans. After its June 1944 liberation, Kiev began a massive reconstruction. The modern government complex surrounded a plush, well-manicured lawn lined with benches, a sanctuary for people seeking a break from the bureaucracy, regardless of what side of a desk they occupied.

We entered the Social Services building, where ten-foot ceilings and wide hallways testified to the government's might. Employees sat at desks cluttered with paper, their old-fashioned typewriters beating a tattoo. I saw no computers. Windows were open to let in fresh air, especially needed in the absence of air-conditioning. American country music played softly over the P.A. I sat while Svetlana disappeared into several offices, returning with paperwork for my signature. She patiently explained the purpose of each document: legal questionnaires probing my fitness to adopt, my financial wherewithal, my willingness to maintain contact with the Ukraine Embassy—and many more that, in a state of sheer overload, I simply signed without understanding. It felt more like we were negotiating an international business contract than creating a family.

In the morning, after another breakfast of Nabs, I got a call from Svetlana who told me that all the paperwork had been completed. She said she would be by in twenty minutes and that I needed to have all my bags packed; she had just spoken by phone with Ilona, who waited in Odessa. When I exited the car at the airport, I naively looked for a skycap to help with my massive suitcases. I quickly learned that in Ukraine, there's no such thing. As Svetlana and I were struggling, an eager young man offered to help—for a gratuity, of course.

There was no boarding gate. Once we exited the lobby we stepped directly onto the tarmac, a short walk from a small jet plane of about a dozen seats. The pre-flight instructions seemed familiar, though I didn't understand a word. There were no children on the flight; most of my fellow passengers were in business attire.

I devoured the orange juice and chocolate candy I was served and stared at the clouds. Lulled by the hum of the engines, I was relaxed, at peace, content to follow this adventure wherever it might take me. I had no fears.

I was startled back to reality by the hard landing of the plane. Sign language enabled me to persuade some strong-looking men to assist me with the luggage: they even summoned a motorized cart for me. We didn't walk to an airport terminal, but across the asphalt to a very tall chain-link fence, through which I saw Ilona's smiling face. I was excited to see her. It felt almost like meeting family.

Ilona's husband deftly weaved us in and out of traffic in the couple's compact Fiat, as I tried to follow Ilona's explanation that she'd arranged housing, contacted various orphanages to schedule visits, and informed the regional social service offices of my intentions. I knew all of this was vital to successfully completing the adoption, yet I just wanted to leave it all in Ilona's hands; I knew she would handle matters appropriately, assure everything was legal and be there to help me choose the children. Still, I listened politely and thanked her for all she was doing.

"We're going directly to Svetta's," she announced next, "where you'll be staying. She's excited to have you staying there," she continued. "Her grandson lives there as well and speaks a little English, but Svetta and her husband do not speak any English. We live in the same apartment complex. It's a nice place and you'll like it. And, Svetta will definitely make you feel right at home."

We pulled up outside three, five-story brick apartment buildings. The buildings were in dire need of repair, both cosmetic and functional. The metal bars on most of the windows were loose and dangling. Vines matted the walls. Some of the brick looked as if it had simply been piled, rather than cemented, in place; I could see no mortar in the joints. Grime discolored the white trim. The yard was black earth studded with only a few dispersed sprigs of grass. I smelled and felt dirt in my nostrils as soon as we left the car. A fine black haze seemed to hang over everything. Shirts, underwear, pants and dresses of various sizes flapped on clotheslines strung between a couple of large trees.

We walked on buckled sidewalks between wooden benches lining the entranceway to each building. The hallways within were unlit and musty. Rusty mailboxes hung in rows. The smell of urine permeated the air. It brought to mind the many low-income projects I have visited during my twenty-plus years in public health, but I reminded myself that staying in a typical Ukrainian home would give me a greater sense of the culture. I didn't want to show up as a tourist, experience carefully packaged "traditional" flavors of the country, and leave with my souvenir children; I felt it important to understand how Ukrainians lived and ate, the nature of their lives. I wanted a personal connection with the country and its people. Ilona had told me that the adoption process might take five to six weeks: I'd have plenty of opportunity to entrench myself.

We rang the bell outside a third-floor apartment and were greeted by a large, effervescent woman of about fifty, with short black hair, twinkling dark eyes, rosy cheeks and pendulous upper arms. She had a tissue in one hand and patted at the sweat rolling down her neck and face; with the other she reached out to steer me into the apartment, chattering non-stop in

Russian. Ilona introduced me to Svetta, her husband, and their six-year-old grandson, Slaviak.

Svetta was not to be deterred by a language barrier. I couldn't help but smile at her evident pleasure at having me as a guest. Speaking incessantly, she kept pointing to my feet and then to a shelf holding a line of shoes and slippers. I suddenly noticed that everyone else was barefoot, and quickly removed my shoes. She beamed.

We walked to the kitchen, where her husband sat with a satisfied smile at the head of a scratched but sturdy wooden table. The room was quite small, the chairs surrounding the table making for a tight squeeze. The floor was linoleum, the cabinets, metal. Everything was spotless. Ilona attempted to exit but Svetta would not let her near the door. It was obvious that here, Svetta was boss, and her hospitality would not be denied. Ilona put up only so much of a fight. The food smelled delicious.

My designated seat was on the bench beside Slaviak. She had prepared big bowls brimming with what I learned was a hot Russian borscht of potatoes and vegetables (though not one beet), and bread slathered with melting butter.

Ilona left Svetta and me to a conversation of hand signals and the Russian-English dictionary. I wiped my brow and sighed to indicate that it was hot. She mimicked fanning herself. At times she pointed to her husband or Slaviak as she spoke, stood up and patted me on the back, or just sat there gushing, while I nodded politely. I pointed to "pretty" in the dictionary and made a sweeping gesture of the apartment. She nodded and smiled. I took a spoonful of the hot stew and rubbed my tummy while saying, "Yum." She grinned and patted herself on the back. The room was busy with laughter. I laughed sometimes simply because she did. I didn't have a clue what she was saying, but she sure was enjoying herself.

As we talked, Svetta kept replenishing our bowls, and I kept eating. I said, at last, "No More." "Nyet, nyet." Svetta, poised over me with her ladle, continued to repeat what I recognized as, "Eat, eat, eat."

When she finally let Ilona leave, Svetta showed me around the apartment. Off one side of the central hallway was a master bedroom crowded by a huge, wooden bed and dresser. A dark blue rug decorated with the zodiac hung on the wall over the headboard. Off the bedroom was a tiny screened porch with a pallet on which Slaviak slept. It was the only spot in the apartment with a consistent breeze. Damp clothes hung from clothesline stretched over the bed.

At the end of the hallway were two rooms, one containing a toilet—and with space for nothing more—and the second contained a tub/shower combination. Off the living room was a screened porch with a door into a small room containing a single bed. This was Slaviak's winter bedroom.

Next came my quarters: the pullout sofa in the living room. Around the room were shelves loaded with books and knick-knacks, a TV and the door to the screened porch. Two windows overlooked the dirt yard out front.

I slept with both windows wide open and lay perfectly still in order to keep my heat level at a minimum. Sleeping without air-conditioning brought back childhood nights in Florida, when I'd desperately push my nose against the screen to capture any breeze that might whisper by. I shifted left and right on the sofa bed, searching for that elusive spot free of poking bars and the inevitable middle furrow. With great relief I found the perfect position and settled into my usual mummy posture. I was eager for the next morning to come.

Shortly after six, I awoke to the chants of a woman outside hawking her wares, Svetta banging around in the kitchen, and friendly conversations among women below my window. I lingered in bed awhile, savoring my novel and anticipating the robust aroma of freshly brewed coffee. There was none, but there was no shortage of breakfast, which consisted of several courses—bread, oatmeal, milk, cucumbers and, not least, tomatoes, which I gathered were a staple at most meals. As Ilona and I were leaving for the day's business, Svetta shoved a bag into my hand. Our lunch. I felt like a school girl running for the bus.

I wore a book bag, suitably enough, though it was filled with hundreds of pages of documents and official forms. Lacking a car, we stood on the curb, Ilona waving at the traffic until a car stopped. She explained where we needed to go and proffered a fare. The driver refused and sped off, but the second agreed to her terms. This, I learned, is an everyday mode of public transportation in Odessa.

"Aren't you afraid that something bad could happen?" I asked Ilona. "I hitchhiked, as we call it, when I was a teenager, but I sure wouldn't do it in today's world."

"Oh no, everyone does it," she replied. "And people need the money, so you can always find a ride."

I sat in the back seat of the stranger's Fiat. The driver was young, tanned and had curly black hair. Once our doors were closed he stomped on the accelerator and zoomed into traffic without regard for cars already there or the screaming and honking of their drivers. He jockeyed the Fiat into any space that opened around us; it felt like we'd entered a stock-car race. The car lacked seatbelts, so I gripped the door handle. Ilona chatted casually with the driver. I realized why Fiats were the car of choice in Odessa: Anything bigger wouldn't fit.

Potholes loomed, creating an obstacle course. The streets devolved in places to dirt, too, quite a surprise in such an urban center, and they were gouged with deep ruts and holes. Our driver reveled in successfully navigating around every barrier put before him, grinning and chuckling at each missed pothole and glancing in the mirror at the plight of cars behind. We could hear them bottoming out in the craters he had managed to avoid. He drafted bumper-to-bumper behind motorists he deemed were traveling too slowly, and demonstrated without hesitation and while looking over at Ilona, that three Fiats could travel side-by-side on a two-lane road.

We roamed through several neighborhoods and over a succession of dusty roadways. The homes around us were small, less than a thousand square feet, and rose from tiny, fenced dirt lots. They were painted in drab browns and grays or weathered bare. Clotheslines and derelict cars cluttered what passed for front lawns and junkers sat abandoned along the road. Barefoot children, many just in their underclothes, dueled with sticks; a few lucky ones had balls they kicked back and forth. Dogs roamed, ribs protruding.

When we pulled into the orphanage, children swarmed us from every direction crying, "Mama, mama" and "Candy," with hands extended for something to eat. Many were in dirty underwear. A good number, girls and boys alike, were shirtless and shoeless.

The mob of children blocked our passage up the sidewalk until Ilona was able to persuade them to go off and play. Three women caretakers sat knitting under large shade trees. They seemed oblivious to our presence.

We found most of the boys in the back yard, digging in the dirt around a twenty-by-twenty-foot concrete slab, once a basketball court but now cracked and weedy. One caretaker sat with a small branch stripped of all its leaves, which I realized was a switch for children caught misbehaving.

The children seemed to be organized into three groups—the controllers, or bosses; the shy "servants" of the bosses; and the clowns. The director introduced me to one boy in the "servant" group. Sasha looked at his feet. He was skinny but not emaciated, and when I knelt to talk with him, he turned his head away. He didn't speak or smile. His body was unresponsive when I hugged him. But the caretaker couldn't say enough good things about him: "He never gets in trouble. He does what he's told to do. He never complains. He's a good boy." She might as well have been describing a used car.

Then we met a clown, and right off, Alec intrigued me. His ribs protruded and his chest was concave, but he flitted from child to child, laughing, and his eyes sparkled with excitement; he seemed intent on making everyone happy. He had blond hair, an elfin face and light blue eyes, which he locked on mine. He patted other children on the back, encouraging them, and when a small boy tripped and fell to the ground, Alec was the first to reach him. With evident care, he held out his hand and helped the boy to his feet. "He's always happy and eager to help. He makes everyone laugh," the caretaker told us. Against all odds in these bleak surroundings, Alec was an optimist, able to both find and share joy. His survival was not a matter of strength, but of heart.

After a twelve-hour day I was grateful for Svetta's warm welcome home. That evening I took my place among the Ukrainian women fanning themselves on the bench outside as they watched the children play. They all wore sleeveless frocks with swooping necks. Their necks were wet with sweat. As they talked they'd lean forward, pull their dresses away, and fan their chests.

Svetta appeared to be the leader of the group and took pains to introduce me to everyone. Presumably she shared my story with them; the women would smile or nod at me, as if we shared a secret.

The next morning we returned to the orphanage to again see Alec. He was energetic enough to power the place. His hair was wet and matted from sweat; his long, thin arms were in constant motion. No wonder there wasn't an ounce of fat on him. He wore red shorts and red and white tennis shoes. The shoes were split at the toe, so that when he walked they flopped like a duck's bill.

He and a trio of friends lined up beside each other, arms over each others' shoulders, and serenaded us loudly, Alec displaying loose and rotten teeth. I felt happy just watching him, to the point that I was almost able to ignore the stench of dirt and urine that followed him and all of the other children.

These kids had been through this routine before. They knew the value of drawing attention, to emerging as an individual among so many faces. My intent was not covert. Yet, Alec gladly pulled other children over to me, encouraging them to talk, shake my hand or hand me a wildflower from the scrubby yard. He didn't seem competitive; rather, he seemed proud of his friends.

I was confident that Alec was the one. I felt connected with him and buoyed by his positive spirit. Yes: I was sure of it. It would be Alec Edwin Welch.

Back at the apartment, Svetta prepared lunch (a cow's heart salad and the ever-present tomatoes and potatoes) while Slaviak and I went outside to play baseball with a small bat and ball I had brought with me. He was unfamiliar with the game and had never seen a glove. The nearest open area for play was a huge concrete slab, evidently an old foundation, next door.

Soon other children who had been playing in the dirt yard slowly ventured nearby to watch this strange activity taking place. They stood at a distance but almost imperceptibly would inch a little closer each time I hit the ball. I intentionally hit a slow ground ball to one of the gawking young boys. He looked at me, then the ball, then me again as if asking what he was supposed to do. He wasn't quite certain he could trust this strange foreign woman who was wearing shorts and tennis shoes, an anomaly among the shift-clad natives. Hesitantly, he bent down and picked up the ball, and then he raised it above his head, with a broad smile.

I applauded. Immediately, all five of his companions joined in with cheers. I motioned for the boy to throw me the ball and with that first pitch our much modified version of street baseball was begun. There were no language barriers that laughter couldn't overcome.

I placed their small hands in the right position around the bat grip and each contact with the ball prompted a jubilant shriek. To their great delight I simulated a pitcher's wind-up, complete with high leg lift, before delivering each easy lob. They rejoiced in trying their hand at pitching and at catching an occasional fly ball.

Amid all of this gaiety I noticed gawking and whispering among the women on the bench. They had undoubtedly never witnessed such unfeminine behavior. Their role was to cook and clean and sit on the bench watching the children; I'd bet none had ever played in the yard or taken up a sport. Such rough, sweaty and dirty activity was left to the men. And most assuredly, none of these women would wear such risqué clothing as shorts. Women wore dresses. For all that, they seemed more curious and doubtful than hostile. I was too strange to dislike.

The next day Ilona and I hitchhiked back to the orphanage to spend more time with Alec. A parade of children followed us to the back yard, hopping and chanting, "Mama, mama." There was craze in the air, a happy excitement. A few boys, anticipating my choice of Alec, congratulated him with pats on the back. Alec, his eyes sparkling, raced towards us. I expected him to go to Ilona—I hadn't said a word to him in his language and he didn't know a word of mine. But to my happy bewilderment he launched himself into my arms, wrapping his bony legs around my waist, his arms around my neck. As I hugged him, I could feel each and every rib.

"I'm shocked," Ilona said as she viewed this energetic tow-head clutching me. "This is most unusual." I later learned that after our last visit Alec had told his caretaker, "I choose her as my mama. I will go to America with her." Who was choosing whom?

That evening Svetta showed a video of Slaviak in a lively Kazachok dance program. This dance was popularized by the Cossacks, who in the days of the tsars lived in the wilds of Ukraine and Russia, subsisted by hunting and fishing, and were considered strong, brave and disciplined fighters; Tennyson portrayed them in "The Charge of the Light Brigade." They developed Kazachok for entertainment, relaxation and competition. It is a lively, boisterous dance meant to show the strength of men and their passion for life and freedom. It celebrates women, by contrast, as soft, graceful and acquiescent. Costumes are bright with lots of red; the Russian word for red is similar to the one for beautiful. A mustached man with salt-and-pepper hair played the accordion with gusto. Consistent with tradition, Slaviak and the other boys, dressed in the Cossacks' famed blousy shirts, red boots and tall hats, demonstrated their athletic prowess with jumps, spins, leaps and the toughest part of the dance: dropping to a squat and alternately kicking their legs out (called knee-bending) while keeping their arms folded and perpendicular to their chests. The girls twirled holding onto their skirts, and bowed their heads so as to avoid looking directly at the boys, as that was considered disrespectful.

Back at the apartment I tried to emulate the dance moves, but grace has not been a word often used to describe me. I twirled, and pitched onto the sofa bed. I held Slaviak's hands as he spun me around and away, and crashed into a table, upsetting a lamp. I tried to knee-bend and wound up taking a seat on the floor. The room was like a sauna and sweat rolled from every pore, but I felt like celebrating.

During dinner of that wonderfully delicious and filling Russian Borscht, Svetta kept pushing a plate of garlic cloves and a mound of salt towards me. I pushed the plate back, oblivious to the lively and insistent monologue with which she was trying to grab my attention. She finally grabbed one of the cloves, and shoving her face just inches from my own, rubbed salt all over the garlic and downed it with one bite. She smiled, picked up another clove, rubbed it in salt (hygiene considerations were minimal) and pushed it towards my lips. Without an alternative, I grabbed the garlic, crammed it in my mouth and chewed as hard and fast as I could.

Tears welled as the clove's robust pungency exploded in my sinuses. I was too stunned to do anything but struggle to breathe; Svetta grabbed my spoon from my hand and fed me several mouthfuls of soup like a baby. Her husband proudly slapped my back and laughed. I'd been initiated. Now I was properly welcomed to the Ukraine.

We returned to the orphanage to look for a younger girl. Children crowded me, hands outstretched, shouting "candy," "American," or "Take me." Ilona would point out those eligible for adoption. Some stood with their heads bowed or shyly turned away. Others shoved their way to the front so I couldn't help but look at them.

In the midst of the jostling and fuss, a caretaker led a six-year-old girl to the pack's rear. I smiled hello to her, and her hazel eyes bored into me, unwavering. She didn't smile or beg or reach out. There was a certain defiance about her, as if she was daring me to reach her well-protected heart. She wasn't afraid of me or moved by me; she betrayed no desire, no dependence.

Yet beneath her stoic facade, I sensed a fragile little girl eager for human connection. I became only vaguely aware of the throng of children around us, the caretaker describing this child as, "very smart," or "a good helper," or "stubborn," or "good at crafts." All of it was background noise: It was as if the only two people in existence at that moment were this girl and me. I had a strange feeling that the two of us were enveloped in a single spirit, one soul. I knew this child. I knew her because I could see me in her.

The staff told me that she'd been returned after six weeks by a previous adoptive family in Italy. The explanation they offered was that she had been physically destructive and violent towards the family. I had a better explanation: she'd been brought back because we were meant to be mother and daughter. We were meant to be a family. This girl, whose name I could not pronounce, would be a Welch. This was our destiny. I was ready. She would be one of God's gifts entrusted to me. All this I knew; and so, it seemed to me, did Alyona Mae Welch.

Chapter 4

The next morning I sat down at the table and Svetta placed a big bowl of cold spaghetti noodles in front of me. I didn't know what to do with them, wondering: Is this breakfast? She then put a pitcher of cold milk on the table, clapped her hands together in front of her and gave me a big grin. I shrugged my confusion. Chattering nonstop, Svetta picked up the pitcher of milk and poured some over the spaghetti, then scooped up a spoonful of sugar and sprinkled it in the bowl. She then stepped back and, bringing her hand up to her mouth, mimed feeding herself. I gingerly took a small bite. What a surprise! In minutes, I had devoured the entire bowl.

Ilona arrived at the door and we prepared to head out for a long day of form-filling and question answering, all parts of the regional adoption process. After expressing some reservations, Svetta had packed our lunches in an insulated lunch bag that I had brought with me from the States. She included a bottle of frozen water to keep our sandwiches cool. She shoved the bag in my hand while delivering a sharp-sounding few words to Ilona.

"What did she say?" I asked.

"She's insulted that you take extra precautions with her food," Ilona replied. "She says no one has ever gotten sick on her food and she's a safe cook."

I didn't think now was a good time to try to conduct a public health lesson on proper food temperatures and food-borne disease. "Just tell her I'm funny that way," I told her, "and blame it on my public health background."

Svetta, unconvinced, waved us towards the door. I left feeling bad that she felt bad, but not feeling bad about my caution. I wasn't about to be lax, not with so much at stake—and with the temperatures climbing too close to 100 degrees.

Our first stop was the regional office, equivalent to a U.S. city's social services department, where we had to initiate the process for Alyona's adoption. It was a huge, three-story stone building with high ceilings, built decades before air conditioning. Our footsteps echoed as we walked the wide marble halls. Old wooden benches, a few with splintered breaks on the seats and legs, lined the walls. A woman and her two toddlers sat on one of the benches, sweat dripping from their chins and beading on their arms. They had distant, catatonic stares.

We stepped into an office where fans pushed the hot air around. There was no music, no laughter, and no tap-tap of computer keyboards. We asked for the supervisor, and a short, balding man presented himself. He wore a well-trimmed mustache and plain, brown-rimmed glasses. His skin was dry and pale. We handed him our paperwork.

He immediately looked me over from head to toe, grimaced at my jeans and said, "You're a doctor. All American doctors are rich. Give me $1,000 and I'll be sure that the paperwork is completed in a timely manner." He folded his hands on his chest and appeared satisfied, no doubt thinking that in my desire to have a child I would quickly comply.

Ilona had prepared me for this possibility, but even so, his brazenness, his confidence, came as a shock. I was insulted about his presumptions about my financial status; clearly, the guy didn't know much about the American public health system. I'd told Ilona that, as a matter of principle, I strongly opposed paying a bribe. She reassured me that, at worst, the process would take a little longer. I was willing to wait.

I looked the man directly in the eyes, and firmly said "Nyet." We walked out.

Next stop: the government lawyer's office. There were no appointments, no number system. In theory, it's first-come, first-served, provided everyone remembers who is ahead of him. We took seats in an airless room, surrounded by peeling paint and dozens of Ukrainians, all sweating under a slow-turning fan. The place reeked of body odor.

Most of our fellow clients sat motionless, staring at nothing. Children sat like zombies on their mothers' laps.

Officials periodically crossed the room from one office to another. They sidestepped the waiting clients as you might detour around a hole in the sidewalk; they didn't devote so much as a glance to us. It was as if the humanity of the office had been obliterated. When the doors to the lawyers' chambers opened we could feel a breath of cool air, ever so slight, that vanished when the door closed.

When a lawyer called for the next client, two women rose. They glared at each other, like boxers trying to psych out an opponent. The older woman, although smaller and in rough physical shape, waved her fist at the stocky, younger woman who faced off with her. The younger woman offered a few gestures of her own. They both spoke with such force that we could see spittle fly from across the room. The lawyer's insouciant manner gave me the distinct impression that such scenes were common, and that he was content to wait for a winner to emerge. After about five minutes, the younger woman stomped furiously back to her seat.

Our turn came after about ninety minutes. I gasped at the pleasure of moving from the oppressively hot waiting room into the lawyer's cool, air-conditioned office. It was painted a cheerful shade of yellow, and all the brighter for the light pouring in from a bank of large windows. Our lawyer was dressed in a well-pressed gray skirt and jacket. A beautiful white pearl necklace hung loosely around her neck. Her appearance was that of a strong, confident professional. She spoke in short sentences, only occasionally looking directly at Ilona.

I could sense there was a dispute when Ilona became more animated and the lawyer simply shrugged her shoulders. Some rule had inexplicably changed since yesterday, it seemed, and we would need to complete new paperwork, and have it approved, to continue the adoption.

Undaunted, Ilona turned us back to the regional office, where she asked to be shown to its lawyer. Without a word, she pulled up a chair beside the lawyer's desk, removed some papers from her folder and began dictating how they should be completed. The lawyer typed feverishly on an old typewriter, its keys sticking, she and Ilona conspiring to overcome an inept system that offered more obstacles than support. They whispered as they tweaked and manipulated the answers to fit the new regulation's legal requirements. Finished papers in hand, I was quickly approved for adoption by the Social Services Board, with the not-so-subtle caveat that I would make an appropriate donation to the orphanage.

On the ride home I was too euphoric to even feel the jarring slams of the potholes and ruts. I was wrenched from this bliss when a cop pulled us over. Although there were no charges, he implied that there could be, unless we produced some cash. Apparently, it was standard operating procedure for these public officials to pad their meager earnings with "contributions" from a grateful citizenry. I tossed some money to our driver to pass to the gentleman.

I was still in an exultant mood when, the next morning, Ilona left me alone for my first visit with the children minus an interpreter. I had filled my backpack with a football, guardian angel doll, magic paper that turned from black to green when you rubbed it, a tape recorder and tapes of children's songs, sunglasses and two rubber stamps of penguins and a smile face.

As soon as Alec saw me, he jumped into my arms and nestled his head on my shoulder. There was so little to him that I feared I would break his ribs if I hugged too hard. He kept saying, "Mama, Mama," as did other children running to gather around us.

I sat Alec on the ground and started unpacking the backpack. His body soon became a walking display of inky penguins and smile faces. When he ran out of skin, he stamped me, the other children, the concrete area, and the football. It was so easy to please him.

A soft tap on my shoulder alerted me that Alyona had sidled up beside me, naked save for a pair of dirty blue shorts. She stood silently, remote, as I gave her a big hug, and then peered without expression into my eyes. I felt as if I were being scanned and saved to a computer. Her time on the streets before the orphanage, the staff told me, had made her highly skilled at reading both people and her surroundings.

When I showed her the smiley stamp her mask broke: Her eyes grew large as a breathtaking smile rearranged her face, showing off white, cavity-free teeth. I gave her a smile-face ring I had on, and she proudly displayed it to all of the children. It was good to see that a child, however strongly armored, still lurked in there. She was especially taken with the guardian angel doll, though I noticed that her handling of it was harsh and abrupt, almost violent. She didn't coddle. She didn't coo.

When I played a tape of children's dance music, Alec instantly began dancing and singing. He grabbed my hands and led me across the dirt. Alyona stood motionless, eyeing the tape player and me with what seemed a mixture of caution and curiosity. I invited her to dance, but she was not yet willing to commit to unrestrained play. She was excited, though, about wearing my sunglasses and being dubbed "cool." That was a word they'd both learn very quickly. She strutted around the yard, confident behind her shades.

We played hopscotch and drew pictures on the concrete with colored chalk. Alec's drawings were doodles, but Alyona produced a pretty sophisticated picture of a house with a roof and four windows, all outlined in red. A stream of smoke was rising from the chimney. There was a red door with a dot for a knob and a winding footpath crossing the yard. The lawn was green and bordered in white flowers with yellow centers. She had drawn a big, bright yellow sun quilled with rays in an upper corner. It was a very cheery picture.

Our serene play ended when four bigger boys descended on the picnic table where we sat and suddenly attacked us, screaming and shouting and ripping the toys from Alyona and Alec. Alyona kicked at them, but they knocked her to the ground. Alec scrambled to pick up all the trinkets they'd thrown in the dirt, to cram them back into the book bag, but the boys snatched them away and threw them out into the yard. I grabbed at the boys, but they overpowered me, shoving me backward until I tripped and sprawled against the picnic table. Alec came to me and took my hand to help me up. Meanwhile the boys shredded Alyona's picture and scattered the pieces over the yard. Alec stood sobbing, holding a few of the scraps, a broken blue crayon and the smiley-face stamp. Alyona, tears streaming down her face, threw dirt in their faces, kicked at them, bit them hard enough to draw blood. I could see two staff members talking under a tree a short ways off, ignoring the melee. I shouted for their help; they didn't respond. Just then, Ilona arrived, shouted at the boys, and pulled them away. I picked up Alyona and Alec and held them. Alec wrapped his arms around my side, rested his head on my chest and wept. Alyona screamed at the boys and strained to get out of my grasp so that she could chase them. It took twenty minutes for them to calm down.

"They're mean boys and don't want anyone to have something they don't," Ilona said, by way of explanation. "They enjoy hurting people. They'll probably end up on drugs and die on the streets."

One day at the orphanage, the children shared "prizes" they'd obtained with persistence and an almost apelike agility. First, we sampled fresh kumquats from tree branches overhanging a neighbor's wire fence, and then sour grapes plucked through the chicken wire. Alyona often led the boys in scaling fences and trees bare-footed, stretching as far as her small body could manage to pluck plums and apples from high branches. The most-desired fruits, perhaps because they were all but unattainable at the orphanage, were tomatoes.

So the next day I brought in eight pounds of tomatoes and thirteen pounds of peaches. The children fell on the food with the excitement that American kids would reserve for free toys. With a cacophony of squeals, laughs and shouts, they devoured every morsel, munching tomatoes like apples and nibbling peach pits bare. They strolled around the orphanage yard smiling, bare tummies stained with tomato juice.

Ilona spent her days sitting at the regional office, waiting for the director to sign the paperwork. Her six-hour shifts in the hallway made her so familiar to the staff that the clerks brought her coffee and cookies and teased that a bed was next. The director ignored her.

After I spent a long day of waiting with her, I came home to Svetta and a home brew called vass, promoted as non-alcoholic but so beer-like that I had my doubts. All day Svetta had simmered several huge pots of grapes and cubes of bread, adding sugar now and then according to taste. Vass was evidently another initiation that I had to pass. Only after I had chugged down the tonic did Svetta pull a bottle of pasteurized milk from the refrigerator, along with a box of cereal; now that I could pass for Ukrainian, I'd earned an American breakfast.

The next morning Svetta led me into the kitchen, eyes bright with excitement, and my bowl of cereal. I began to pour milk on what looked like corn flakes. Svetta waved her arms and shouted. She wrenched the milk from my hand and pointed her finger at me. I was totally flummoxed. She poured the milk into a pan and warmed it up before I was allowed to proceed. This was not the time to object, I realized, and ate my breakfast with enthusiasm.

After fourteen days, the director signed the adoption papers, foregoing his demands for a bribe. He said nothing and avoided eye contact. His staff sat quietly at their desks, pencils in hand and paperwork before them; yet I caught a few stolen glances my way. Some could not contain sly smiles, which they struggled to hide by turning their heads. The tension in the air was palpable. When the director handed me the finalized papers, he kept his head bowed, not unlike an embarrassed competitor who has lost a match. I reached out to shake his hand; he begrudgingly responded with a limp, cold handshake. "Spasiba," I said—*thank you*—and grasping my hard-won approvals, strode quickly to the exit. It was a test of my restraint; I was exhilarated and felt more like doing a victory dance, pointing a finger at the director and repeatedly shouting, "I won! I won!"

When Ilona and I then went to the lawyer's office, I learned that she'd kept a secret from me for several days. Government officials in Kiev had decided that they would only grant me permission to adopt one child. Ilona had not mentioned this, as she'd hoped to persuade the officials to change their minds—and, indeed, she had succeeded. In the interim, however, the local police had arbitrarily decided that no adopted child could leave the country until ten days after leaving the orphanage—double the time required by the previous law.

That night I had a very strange and powerful dream. I was loading piles of luggage into the trunk of my car. Suitcases were jutting from the trunk. The lid was open wide to accommodate them. I found a long rope and was frantically securing the luggage and lid. I then loaded Alyona and Alec in the car and drove away. When I woke, I wondered if I was more anxious about the adoption process than I realized. Parenthood was coming at me fast now. I was still devoted to and engaged in my public health career. Could I simultaneously be competent at both? Was I taking on more than I could handle? My worst fear was to prove incompetent. Yet I knew I was meant to adopt these two children, so I needed to abandon this unnecessary "luggage" of concern to make room for my new family.

⌒⌒

The bright sun highlighted the red in her auburn hair. She held her right hand over her forehead to shield her eyes from the glare as she searched the crowd for me. I shouted and waved, and a broad grin swept over her freckled face as she walked towards me, dragging a giant suitcase. "Oh my God, I made it!" Laura cried. "I'm still a bit overexcited and overwhelmed. And oh so very glad to finally be here."

Taking her elbow I steered her towards the car. "I've never done anything like this before, especially all by myself," she said, with the manic delivery of the overtired. "I've never had to navigate through foreign anything much less airports when I'm trying to catch a flight. Everyone was nice, but I was so uncomfortable just trusting all these strangers to help." She took a deep breath and dived back in. "I kinda was worried that I'd be stranded in Kiev but yet I knew you wouldn't let that happen. Thank you ever so much for having Svetlana meet me. She's such a nice lady and had a sign with my name on it so I could find her. The trip was so long that when I saw Svetlana she looked like an angel. Then when she took me to the plane it was so much smaller than the other one. Oh my God, I just knew something would happen. I have to let Greg know that I arrived OK."

I took advantage of another breath. "We're going by the house so you can settle in. You can e-mail Greg from there." I brought her up to speed on Ilona's progress with the bureaucracy. "I can't tell you how much I appreciate your doing this," I told her.

We turned into the apartment complex. "Welcome to your Ukraine home," I said. Svetta was bubbling with enthusiasm when I introduced them, and immediately embarked on a tour of the apartment that ended in Laura's small room. As I glanced around, I pondered how she managed to rate a bed and an actual bedroom while I survived in the living room. But I had long learned not to question Svetta's decisions!

Two days later—August 12, 1999—Ilona informed us that we needed to get ready for an adoption party at the orphanage. Tradition held that on adoption day, the new parents brought sweets, cakes, candy and soda for all 165 children, champagne and sweets for the teachers, and wine, candy and flowers for the director. We arrived at the orphanage to a greeting from two beaming and excited children, both freshly bathed and wearing clean clothes for their passport photos.

The court building was actually a residential apartment complex in which several rooms were devoted to legal affairs. The grassless yard was the playground for filthy, half-clothed children who contented themselves, in the absence of swings or slides, with digging holes or climbing trees. Their clothes were stained with urine. An old man with a scraggly beard sat alone on one of the concrete benches. His slender, yellow-stained fingers held the unlit butt of a cigarette, which he occasionally brought to his lips. He was engaged in a lively conversation with no one, and seemed totally blind to his surroundings.

The building itself was in major disrepair. Parts of the roof were missing. The ivory paint had turned a smoky gray with age and neglect. Clothes were draped over balcony railings. I could not believe that such a decrepit wreck could be home to important judicial decisions. As I stood gaping, twelve handcuffed criminals were escorted by police past the dirty children and into the building.

The interior was no better. An interpreter took the children away for their passport photos while Ilona and I sought our hearing before a judge. The halls smelled like those of a low-income housing project in America. Spiders and their webs occupied the corners. Fist-sized dust balls were scattered all over the floors. Dim lighting amplified the rather dank atmosphere. We climbed a rickety spiral staircase to the second floor.

The judge's office was air-conditioned. We sat in metal chairs while the judge, a friendly and gracious woman, questioned me; she was concerned about two children moving in with a single mom, and the availability of people to help me. And she made repeated references to Alyona's tantrums: She wanted to be sure I understood that Alyona frequently bit, kicked, hit or threw things when she didn't get her way. Alyona refused to discuss specifics, or had repressed the memory, of what had happened to her on the streets, but her violent reactions certainly seemed to indicate that this young girl had endured unspeakable abuse and had learned to fight—-to survive— and learned it very well. The judge reminded me that an Italian family had adopted her, only to bring her back because of her violent behavior. The judge suggested that helping this child heal, learn to trust and adopt gentle and acceptable behavior would challenge a couple, let alone a single parent. She seemed more concerned about me than Alyona. I reassured her that I was aware of the difficulties ahead and knew without reservation that we were meant to be a family. I was committed to make it work. I was not blindly adopting this child; I was faithfully forming my family as I believed I had been called to.

The judge wished me the best and signed the approval papers: A few simple gliding movements of her pen, and I was a mother. As I walked from the building, I felt oddly detached from what had just transpired, as if I had just signed a mortgage for a new home, bought a new car, made out a will.

I had no sense of motherhood, no excited thumps of the heart at finally being a parent; I had no visions of playing in the park, making cookies or evenings spent watching children's movies. I felt more ownership, obligation and responsibility, a profound sense of their dependence on me; it was up to me to protect these children, to help them recover from their pasts, and to feel good about themselves. I had absolutely no idea how I would do these things. But I was sure that I would find a way.

⌒⌒

First, however, I had adult battles to wage. At the registrar's office, a clerk insisted that Article 53 of the Ukrainian Adoption Codes required me to give the name of an American father who could be placed on Alyona's and Alec's birth certificates. The fact that I was single and lived alone seemed to have no relevance. It was quite plain that no birth certificate would be issued without a father's name.

At the registrar's suggestion, we arrived at a solution: I would lie! I supplied a fictional name, Jonathon Michael Welch, as the father of the pair. The name was legally recorded and printed on both children's certificates.

When we arrived at Svetta's apartment together, Alyona and Alec were desperate to touch, smell or push everything in sight, and to do it fast; three adults and seven year-old Slaviak were unable to keep up with them. Alyona smelled, sprayed or poured all the perfumes she found and Alec pushed every button on every apparatus—TV, radio, tape player. It was easy to understand their excitement, curiosity and incredible sense of freedom.

Then the mood shifted. Alyona started pulling books down from the shelves, flipping a few pages, and tossing them to the floor. Svetta reached out to stop her, but Alyona was quick and ducked away. Alec grabbed a small glass frog from the shelf and, shouting Alyona's name, tossed it to her over Svetta's head. Alyona missed it and the statuette tumbled under the sofa bed. I lunged for it, but Alyona got to it first and, laughing at me, threw the frog to Alec. Slaviak intercepted it and gave it to Svetta, who was already moving items from her lower shelves to the upper ones, and concurrently shouting to Laura and me. We didn't understand her, and had our hands full, besides—-

we were trying to anticipate the children's next moves so we could keep them from throwing or breaking anything else. We shouted back and forth across the room—"Alec's messing with the TV." "Look out behind you, Alyona's racing to the door." "Duck!"

Svetta's face was red with anger. She shouted at Alec and Alyona, who ignored her. She raised her fists at me. I didn't know what she wanted me to do. I didn't know what I <u>could</u> do. I shrugged my shoulders and told her I was sorry as a book whizzed through the air between us. I grabbed Alec as he tried to escape the room.

The bedlam lasted about an hour and then, without warning, Alec and Alyona suddenly sat down on the sofa bed, clapped joyfully and rolled around on the mattress, laughing. They'd had a marvelous time. Svetta, Laura, Slaviak and I were drenched with sweat. An exhausted Svetta fanned herself while rocking. I slumped on the floor, where Laura joined me. "They're a challenge," she observed, straight-faced. "Well," I said, "it's certainly not your typical motherhood experience."

For the rest of the afternoon, Slaviak and Alec played politely with building blocks and cars while Alyona enjoyed "tea" and dressing up the dolls I had brought her. There was no hint of what had prompted the chaos; even after Svetta spoke with them she shrugged her shoulders to indicate that she had no answer. That evening, Svetta decided that it would be best for Alyona and Slaviak to sleep on the large back porch which adjoined Svetta's bedroom. Svetta evidently thought that Alyona was the main troublemaker, and needed "a strong Russian mother" nearby. Alec would sleep with me.

Except that all night Alec jumped on the bed, screamed, hollered and cried. He could not be soothed. He could not be distracted with stories or play. Svetta couldn't get him to tell her what was wrong; eventually, she shook her head and went to bed. He had no off button. He was neither destructive nor angry, and he didn't seem interested in sleeping on the porch with Alyona and Slaviak. He just wanted to jump on the bed and scream. I was frazzled and tired. I worried what the other residents of the apartment complex would say, for they surely could hear him. Would they kick us out? Would Svetta ask us to leave? I sat up all night, watching him, to ensure he didn't hurt himself. How I wished that I could better communicate with him.

Several times Alyona dashed through Svetta's bedroom, hoping to join Alec in the living room, but each time Svetta snagged her and returned her to the porch. I could hear our hosts' stern reprimands to her. Whatever they said, worked: Alyona quit her escape attempts, and stayed put for the rest of the night. I was grateful that I didn't have to deal with both of the children's antics at the same time, but worried, too. What would I do when it was just the children and me at home? How would I be able to deal with them, when I couldn't even speak to them in words they understood?

The next morning I was exhausted. Alec acted as if he had slept the night through. Thank goodness our plan for the hot and muggy day was an excursion to the Black Sea. Following a thirty-minute trolley ride, we trekked across a weedy moor liberally sprinkled with boulders and gravel fields, which made the footing precarious. For me, anyway—Alyona and Alec sprinted beyond the field to the beach proper, then across the coarse and gravelly sand to the dark, seaweed-choked sea. They splashed and giggled, oblivious to the grime that the water left on their skin.

When the sea's novelty dissipated, they took notice of the attractions on a nearby patch of scruffy lawn—a swinging chair ride, its chains rusty and old, and a squadron of dilapidated children's pedal cars. It wouldn't compare to our own boardwalk amusement parks, but the carnival atmosphere, especially the snow cones and cotton candy, filled the kids with excitement. They ran from one vendor to another, entranced by watching one swirl cotton candy onto a paper cone and another scoop ice into balls, then flavor it with colorful syrups. My instinct was to not give them the sweets for fear that it would make them even more hyper; yet vivid memories of their uncontrollable rage the day before prompted me to give them whatever they wanted just so I wouldn't have to deal with such an outburst in this very public venue. I was afraid to say nyet.

They especially liked the pedal cars. Alec's driving, however, left much to be desired: He spent most of his time behind the wheel with his head turned to the rear. I leaned down and did my best to steer his car away from pedestrians, rides, and vendor pushcarts. The grounds were not well cared-for, and were bumpy with mounds of dirt and scattered gravel. I tripped on trash and empty bottles, and once, struggling to keep my balance, lost my grip on the steering wheel. Alec laughed and accelerated, and aimed at full speed toward a new-looking car in the parking lot as I dashed after him, shouting and waving my hands. At the last moment he made a sharp turn to the right and rammed into a small fence. As he pulled the car away, its entire rear half fell off, exposing the back axle. Alec quickly ran to get Alyona to show her what he'd done. Together they examined the wreckage. Alec stood a little taller and straighter, obviously proud of his accomplishment, and Alyona patted him on the back. I sheepishly returned the pieces to the vendor, who didn't seem the least bit surprised or upset.

The next few days brought moments not nearly so hilarious, episodes that presaged hundreds of others in the years to come. We were at a crowded outdoor flea market. Clothes were among the items for sale and as there were no changing rooms, customers would pull on clothes over whatever they were already wearing—or, in the case of a few bold and immodest shoppers, simply undressed amid the crowd.

Alyona and Alec were especially taken with the toys for sale. Visibly upset when told he could not have one, Alec would clutch it close to his chest, so that it had to be pried away from him—at which point he'd scream for a few seconds until he spotted a new and more intriguing toy.

Alyona, on the other hand, spied a stuffed bear and instantly wanted it. It was far too big to pack or carry on the plane. But that made no difference to her, even when Svetta and Ilona explained the situation: Alyona refused to return the bear to the vendor. The more we tried to take the bear from her, the stronger she held it. When, at last, I was able to break her hold and return the bear to the shopkeeper, Alyona went berserk. She kicked dirt in my face and began hitting me with her fists. She screamed loudly at Svetta and Ilona. She grabbed other items from the vendor's shop and tried to dash to other booths, and when I grabbed her to keep her close she bit my hands and spit in my face. I picked her up by the waist and holding her as high as I could weaved through the crowd, which quickly parted to give us more room. She pulled my hair, kicked my side and beat on my arms. I kept moving towards a more secluded spot near a tree, and once there, sat on the ground, put her on my lap and crossed my legs over hers to pin them down. I crossed her arms in front of her and held them tightly against her chest. She threw her head backwards, butting me hard in the face. I quickly moved my head from side to side to avoid further blows. She kept up the attack for about ten minutes and then, without explanation, simply stopped, her body relaxed, her breath calm and even.

My trust was shaken. We remained still for a couple of minutes before I dared to loosen my hold on her. She stood and walked back to the market as if nothing had happened. I sat there in the dirt for a while, stunned. What had just happened? It was as if a switch had been thrown in her, both to start the outburst and end it. When I returned to the shop, I found Alyona smiling and showing off bright red and yellow barrettes she had found.

Ilona reported that Alyona had screamed "very bad words," some "too bad for me to repeat." She asked whether I was okay.

"I'm still recovering," I told her. "I can see that it will take a lot of work and time." Alyona's behavior reminded me of movies I'd seen about Helen Keller; blind and mute, she'd behaved like a wild animal, violent and belligerent. The comforting part of the comparison, of course, was that she was able to get better, and went on to become an inspiration.

Back at Svetta's, Laura and I were in constant motion in our efforts to keep Alyona from hurting herself, someone else or the apartment. The child's eyes were wild with rage during her tantrums. She seemed driven by an inner fury that was disconnected from the tangible world around her. We tried to calm her outbursts with gentle talking, to no avail. Svetta, belt in hand, wanted to spank her into submission, but I intervened. We weren't going to go that route, though I often had to use the pediatric restraining hold that I'd tried at the market. Her head-butts made it apparent that she was no novice: She would bend her head far forward, for maximum momentum and impact when she flung it back at my face. I usually dodged these maneuvers, but when I miscalculated, Alyona's head would thud into the bridge of my nose, blood would flow, and I'd reflexively let go of her arms; later, as I held ice to my face, I'd catch Alyona and Alec laughing and pointing at me.

Laura's usual jubilant demeanor was quickly muted. Alyona's fits tended to last about forty minutes, and to end when she had physically exhausted herself—or, sometimes, when Svetta's booming Russian commands punctured the caul of madness that enveloped her. Then, in an instant, she'd become docile, politely helping to clean the mess she'd made. She'd again be a playful child of six, as if the episode had never occurred. Alec vacillated from trying to calm Alyona, to conspiring in the mayhem, to standing in mute awe at the magnitude of his new sister's blow-ups.

As we struggled to make sense of all this, Ilona worked to overcome Ukraine's inevitable and multitudinous bureaucratic snags, while circumventing rules and capitalizing on old connections. Our case was shuffled from office to office, subjected to ever-changing rules and requirements, or treated with utter indifference. The state was only a little more predictable than Alyona.

At last came the final form, the last required signature, and the time for us to leave Odessa for our complicated journey home. We set out in the middle of a hot and moonless night—even the rain made us sweat. Our luggage was strapped to the top of the car. The children were asleep, exhausted from a tantrum that erupted when we were packing, over Alyona not being able to sleep where she wanted.

I was tense, anticipating a nine-hour drive with five of us crammed into a subcompact. And I was saddened by leaving Ilona and Svetta: I had really grown attached to them and would miss their support and laughter. They had become friends and confidantes. Now I was venturing into the unknown world without them. Tears mixed with the raindrops on my cheeks.

The road to Kiev was narrow, unmarked and unlit, a poorly paved two-laner. The rain intensified, its drumming on the roof lulling me into a half-waking trance. I reflected on my journey thousands of miles from home—how I'd pinpointed Odessa on a world map back in Virginia. I wondered at my willingness to set aside my staunch independence, to place my life and future in many strangers' hands. I stroked the children sleeping beside me, smiled at the reality of their soft flesh and restful breathing. I peered at Laura's silhouette in the front seat, and wept in gratitude for her help, her generosity.

We passed by a number of truck stops, consisting of large canopies under which travelers could sit on folding chairs, out of the rain, and buy snacks from vendors. There were no bathrooms. In the shadows I could faintly see the backs of several men relieving themselves.

Alec's calls of nature were easily answered beside the car, but Alyona and I posed more of a challenge. On one stop, we tramped in the rain to the roadside and fell into a ditch, invisible in the dark. Our feet sank in the loose mud. We arrived in Kiev dirty, damp and disheveled, drove to a pre-arranged rendezvous point, and met another stranger who'd play a significant role in our lives: Tatiana.

Tall, black-haired and commanding, she strode to us, promptly dismissed our driver and started us into the bureaucratic maze of buying airline tickets to Warsaw, our next way station. When Tatiana spoke, people straightened in their seats and listened; a process that normally would take days, she completed in about three hours.

How welcoming her meticulously neat home felt when we arrived there. There were flowers in every room, books along the walls, and her small but adequate kitchen was light and airy, its windows facing the playground four stories below. The larger bedroom, which she shared with her husband, Vladimir, was of modest size and free of clutter; only a jewelry box sat on the dresser. The second bedroom was small and crowded with a sofa and cot for our stay. The bathroom brought an unqualified delight: Unlike Svetta's place, hot water was a reality at all hours of the day.

When I exited the bathroom, Tatiana was lecturing Alec, who stood at attention, nodding to her every word. She was decreeing that all visitors, even boys, sat on the toilet. No standing was permitted. They had raised their two boys with that rule, and everyone using the bathroom since had followed it, too.

The next morning at breakfast when Tatiana ordered Alec to sit up straight, I found myself doing it, and saw that Laura complied as well. When she told us it was time to leave, we lined up like sheep, ready to follow her lead. Her style invited no dissent, sought no consensus; she expected order, obedience, efficiency. Like children, Laura and I obeyed.

We learned that Vladimir had left home at 3:30 AM to take a place in line at an office where we needed to complete some paperwork. When we arrived a little before nine, we saw Vladimir stood first in line. As we waited, we heard horror stories from those behind us of inexplicable delays, newly imposed rules, and predictions that our paperwork would take days or weeks to complete. Tatiana set out to prove the predictions wrong. Through sheer boldness, she connected with the driver for the official in charge of all the paperwork, and with a mere $50 bribe, the process was greased to a mere three days.

Tatiana pulled off her next feat at the clinic where Alyona and Alec had to be examined. We arrived to an overflowing waiting room and the secretary's assurance that over two hundred persons were present, and, of course, service was all first-come, first-served. That only energized Tatiana. Rod-straight, she marched to the clinic's door. A nurse and the secretary watched with mouths agape, but neither tried to stop her as she pushed the door open and walked through. After a moment she reappeared to wave us in. We emerged thirty minutes later with the completed examination forms in hand.

Four days into our stay in Kiev, I was physically and emotionally exhausted. Alyona was proving herself a smart and strategic manipulator. She would talk with a kindly voice to Tatiana and help her dry dishes after meals, but if I walked by, she'd stick her tongue out at me, then say something to Tatiana in a sweet, syrupy voice. Such an angel. At other times, after first checking to be sure Tatiana wasn't looking, she would, without provocation, dash up to Laura or me and kick us in the shins, or grab a book I'd be reading and try to tear out the pages. When we tried to stop her, she resorted to biting, spitting, pulling hair, screaming, hitting and kicking. I felt like I was in a cage with a wild animal. Alec would join in to "protect" Alyona. He would try to pull us to the floor, tear at our clothes, beat on our backs. That such small children could be so aggressive or strong was a revelation. Tatiana would shout, however, and the children would run to her. Then she would hold her finger up at me, "You don't know how to be a mother," she said. "You should never have children."

This had me stressed, to say the least. So did Tatiana's controlling nature: After each meal, she ordered the children put their hands in the air and go to the bathroom to wash up; when I poured ketchup on the children's food, she'd tell me when to stop. She wouldn't let me cut the children's food, insisting that she do it. When I told Alyona and Alec that they'd had enough candy, she gave them more. When Laura and I played with the children on the monkey bars she bellowed out of the kitchen window to get off of the equipment, then came down to reprimand us in front of the kids. When Laura and I each held Alec's hands and let him jump up and down between us, Tatiana grabbed our hands and told us to stop. If I protested, Tatiana dismissed me with a wave. "This is my house," she said, "and I am in charge." Unfortunately, I was totally dependent on her. She could make the adoption happen or stop it cold; it was up to her to get us out of the country. I didn't even know how to call Ilona for help. And Tatiana's coldness worried me. I imagined that if angered, she would feel no compunction about putting us out with nowhere to go. I simply had to endure her. It's only because Laura was there with me, and we could commiserate and support each other, that I was willing and able to grit my teeth and move on.

At meal time she fed Laura and me, then dismissed us to the living room while she, Vladimir, Alyona and Alec ate together. If I tried to stay, she'd push me out. She only had four kitchen chairs, she noted; but when I suggested that she and Vladimir eat separately so that Laura, the children and I could eat together, she vetoed the idea. "Nyet, nyet," she said. "It is good for the children to eat with us so we can all talk. They don't understand you so they are scared of you. We are like family."

When we returned from excursions, she and Vladimir immediately scooped the children up and gave them a scrubbing, taking care to keep the bathroom neat. They conferred with me on nothing. They demeaned Laura and me at every turn. There was no way I could win these battles so it was easier, for the moment, to give in.

Was it any surprise that the children were hellions, especially around Laura and me? At the Department of Foreign Ministries, Tatiana stood in line while Laura and I watched the children outside. Alyona led Alec in chanting some choice English words: "Fuck, fuck, bitch, bitch." I had no idea where they had learned these bits of their new tongue, but imagined that the orphanage had been a fine place to expand one's vocabulary. They ran, weaving among moving cars, and launched attacks with sticks on Laura and me. While one distracted us with punches from the front, the other would attack from the rear, kicking and pulling our hair. Eventually, both children escaped and ran inside to Tatiana, huddling by her legs. Tatiana brushed Laura and me away. I leaned against a wall and glared at Alyona clinging to Tatiana, practically shouting in my head: "I can hardly wait until we are on my turf and you can no longer play these silly games. Then the real work will begin. You are in for quite a shock, little girl."

One evening I was playing tickle games with the children, provoking them to squeal with delight. Tatiana shouted for us to stop and condemned me for playing such games. Then she burst into tears and abruptly fled to her bedroom. Alyona went to her to kiss her goodnight; Tatiana pushed her away.

Vladimir stayed up and played games with the children, out of Tatiana's sight. At bedtime he was leading Alyona into their bedroom, where they'd set up her cot, when she started crying. She was promptly banished.

So the four of us settled in for the night. Due to the children's bedwetting, we had been evicted from the second bedroom to a mattress on the floor of the living room, minus sheets or blankets. We squeezed onto it, at which point Laura and I were savagely attacked for two hours.

"Why are they so angry at us?" I asked Laura. "Why doesn't Tatiana help? She hears the screaming and knows what they are saying." I was angry, in pain and totally baffled. I didn't know what to do. I was in a fight for survival; but my foe, a six-year old, was more seasoned and adept than I. Oh, how I longed for Ilona or Svetta. And oh, how I looked forward to leaving.

The children continued their onslaught. They'd strategize in Russian before Alyona pulled out clumps of my hair and with a laugh showed it off to

Alec. They added new bite marks to our arms. They screamed, slapped and kicked. We tried restraining holds. We tried ignoring them. We tried gentle talk. We tried a cheek slap. Nothing worked, until finally, sheer exhaustion overcame all of us. We woke the next morning with numerous bruises and an announcement from Tatiana: "The children are too destructive," she said, "so I don't want them in the house all day."

Without telling us where we were headed, she led us out to the car, and we ventured to a sprawling historical park, recreating Kiev as it was three hundred years before. Tatiana's complaints about my parenting were on the rise: As we set off into the park, she fixed on Alec's shoes, which were the sandal type shoes worn by many American children. She was very animated and loud in complaining to Vladimir about how inappropriate the shoes were for the day's activities. I knew nothing! I was no parent! I had no skills! I prayed that God would put glue on the shoes so Alec wouldn't trip even once all day.

It was a wonderfully fun excursion among thatched homes and music of many years passed, of racing on footpaths and lots of laughter. Tatiana spent most of the day quite a distance ahead of us, so Laura and I were able to create a playful environment without interference. It was a much-needed break from our tension and fear that the children would erupt: Here they seemed happy and I felt relaxed and spontaneous; I reveled in the park's refreshing air, chuckled at the children's antics and wrapped myself in the serenity of this idyllic place. Our troubles seemed distant. I experienced a renewed optimism that this strange little family would heal.

The peace ended when we got back to Tatiana's. Laura and I were told to take the children outside while she prepared dinner. Once we were away from Tatiana I could see a change come over Alyona's face. Her eyes acquired a taunting fire. Her mouth and jaw became rigid. Her behavior went from playful to planned and controlling.

A whisper to Alec, and they were calling us names, throwing rocks and sand at us, and biting or kicking when we drew too close. Exasperated, I picked up Alyona and carried her yelling and kicking up the four flights of stairs to the apartment. When I explained what had happened, Tatiana gave Alyona treats. It was as if she were being rewarded for her misbehavior.

Not only that, but she punished the good: When Vladimir played with the children that evening, bouncing them on his knee, Tatiana yelled at him to stop.

Thank goodness, the paperwork was completed in record time and the day of departure finally arrived. That morning after I dressed Alec, Tatiana stormed into the room and removed the shirt I had put on him, replacing it with the two shirts she had selected. I grabbed at her hands to stop her, asking: "What are you doing?"

"You don't know anything about dressing boys," she answered. "I know how to do it." I released my grip on her wrist. It just wasn't worth a battle. We'd soon be free of this treatment; that was far more important than whatever shirt Alec wore.

These had been a brutalizing four days, physically and emotionally. The respect for me that Ilona and Svetta had fostered in the children had been destroyed and replaced with ridicule. Tatiana had been necessary for our escape from Ukraine, but it would take time and effort to fully escape <u>her</u>.

Our departure was without hugs or tears. We exchanged a business-like handshake, at which time Tatiana said, "God be with you."

Chapter 5

Our mission in Warsaw was to obtain the children's visas as quickly as possible—and, we hoped, before our hotel evicted us or the police were called. We had a small, two-bed room in the heart of the city; our strategies included maximum use of the TV, frequent and energetic bubble baths, in-room games, blowing bubbles, eating in, and venturing only as needed to the embassy.

As much as I avoided McDonald's at home, I was eternally grateful for its presence two blocks from the hotel and the fact that it served breakfast, lunch and dinner. It didn't hurt that we could order by simply pointing at a picture.

But returning with our first lunch, I opened the door to find bed linens and clothes strewn over floor, lamps and bed posts, the TV blaring, and water seeping from under the bathroom door. I could hear Alyona and Alec giggling behind it. Laura sat in a stupor on the bed, her blouse hanging low over her left shoulder.

When I asked what had happened she burst into tears. In the forty minutes I'd been gone, the children had launched repeated attacks at her, throwing anything they could grab, taking turns with frontal assaults to enable the other to get up to all sorts of destructive mischief. As if running a gauntlet, she had made it to the bathroom, where she had filled the tub with bubble bath and blown bubbles at the children to entice them into the tub. Naked and covered with bubbles from head to toe, the children now appeared, over the wet, slippery floor, drawn by the aroma of cheeseburgers and fries. They didn't resist being bundled in towels and sitting on bed for a "picnic."

After dinner, the children's energy remained in high gear, and a warm, beautiful evening beckoned. We strolled among Warsaw's versatile architecture—a bit of Gothic, a bit of Renaissance, a bit of modern—and enjoyed the casual atmosphere. There was cheer in the air, rich laughter. The sidewalks were crowded with young adults enthusiastically perusing the wares offered at the vast array of outdoor kiosks bunched along the walkway.

And Alyona and Alec followed suit, only with a lot more vigorous an inspection. Alec wanted to see how everything worked. Alyona wanted to try everything on. Four hands were barely enough to contain them. They would snatch up all they could hold, and scurry off with huge grins, only to be confused and distraught when we required them to return the swag. The abundance of vendors and selections, though, meant they had little time for anger; there was always another booth. Their laughter was a balm.

The next day at the embassy, I was told that the tax forms I'd mailed in, a necessary prerequisite to getting the children's visas, were missing. An embassy worker reassured me that I could complete some new forms, that they'd be sent to the IRS computer system in London, and I could probably be on my way within five days.

"Five days would be an eternity," I cried, watching Laura's eyes widen. "Surely there's another way." After a little negotiation, the embassy staff agreed to my having my IRS paperwork faxed from the States. I hoped my accountant in Virginia would be able to accommodate me, though it was six in the morning back home. I told the official I'd make a call. "The closest phone you can use is two blocks away at the Sheraton," the worker said.

The children were playing calmly in the toy box so Laura agreed to stay while I speed-walked to the phone. My accountant was also a friend, and maintained her office at home. She faxed my tax forms immediately. Feeling somewhat cocky at how smoothly that had gone, I strolled back to the embassy.

I arrived to turmoil. As soon as the door had closed behind me, Alyona had hurled toys at everyone in the room, Alec joining in. Laura, reinforced by other patrons, had tried to stop them, but had been violently attacked by both. The other patrons had been ushered out of the room; the embassy staff looked on from behind high counters and locked doors. Laura, double-teamed, was overwhelmed.

I clamped the restraining hold on Alyona while shouting to the staff that my information was being faxed. After twenty minutes, completely sweat-soaked, Alyona was too exhausted to continue struggling. At about the same time, the staff told us to return in two hours for our visas.

Away from the embassy, Alyona was like a different child. She pointed to birds and giggled at squirrels. She danced to music spilling onto the sidewalk from the stores we passed and hugged a thank you for her lunch. She didn't lack remorse for her earlier behavior; she displayed an almost total lack of acknowledgement that anything had happened. Alec returned to his joyous, affectionate self. Laura and I remained baffled and watchful, expecting the trouble at any moment.

We returned to the embassy and took our place in line behind four other people. A security guard called our name and then escorted us into a completely empty room. After re-locking the door so no one else could enter behind us, he stood guard, tall and erect, glaring. The entire staff was devoted to completing our papers; no other patrons would be permitted into the office until we exited. It was certainly an odd way to obtain red-carpet treatment. Our visas in hand, we were escorted not only from the office but off the premises.

PART II

A Rough Beginning

Chapter 6

Four o'clock came all too slowly. Bleary-eyed passengers made their way to their assigned seats. Those few who spoke did so in hushed tones, preserving the illusion that we were players in a dream. We seated ourselves with both relief and trepidation. We were in the rearmost seats on the plane's right side. Flight attendants were already bustling in the galley behind us, beside a large exit door.

The children were awed by the sheer size of the craft and pointed at the non-Russian persons they deemed most interesting—black people with dreadlocks, Indian women wearing saris, Asian businessmen. They laughed and covered their ears when the plane took off and clamored to catch glimpses of cars, people and buildings out the window. Alyona had a squeal of a laugh that instantly provoked me to join her, even when I had no idea what it was that amused her, and Alec's enthusiasm for touching everything and interacting with everyone around him made me want to be a child again. In these joyous, playful moments I was enthralled to experience the world through their eyes. It was refreshing to feel the wonder of flight without worry about connections or cost, to feel our craft's upward thrust and to marvel at the planes on the ground, the people, trucks and buildings that seemed to shrink as we climbed. To see puffy clouds that seemed soft but solid, like cotton balls, but which proved, when we flew through them, to be more like fog. Ah, what children can teach us.

I convinced myself that I was unwittingly bred to parent Alyona and Alec. By the grace of God, and environmental influences—eldest daughter, strongly encouraging and optimistic parents, an ever-present can-do spirit—I was certain that I possessed the necessary traits for the challenge before me: self-confidence, adaptability, a spirit of adventure, persistence, resilience and a complete trust in my intuition. Let me offer a few examples.

When I was a teenager, my father bought a 1948 Studebaker Champion sedan from our next-door neighbor. He intended that this would be the car used, in turn, by the five of us children, and had it re-painted a dark blue at the local vocational school. The car was a classic, with a mohair interior, three on the column, and a six-cylinder, 169-cubic-inch engine that cranked out 85 horsepower. By the time I turned sixteen, it badly burned oil and the steering required muscle.

My older brother had taken his driving test on the Studebaker. My parents tried to persuade me to take mine on their 1959 Pontiac Bonneville, which they figured would be a lot easier. The Bonneville had power steering, power brakes, turn signals, air conditioning, and an automatic transmission, all of which the Studebaker lacked. But I decided that if this was going to be my car for driving, I should be able to pass the test in it. Hour after hour I practiced parallel parking in the Studebaker. In Orlando, Florida, in July 1962, came my reckoning.

Parallel parking was the last part of the test. I pulled up even with the front car. Then as I slowly backed up I used both hands to turn that wheel with all my might to the right. I put one hand over the other, tugging with determination and daring that wheel to slip out of my now wet-with sweat palms. Sweat ran down the nape of my neck and into my eyes, but I showed no anxiety or tension. When I was content that the car was parked properly, I stopped, turned off the key, sighed and sat upright at attention with my hands resting at the two and ten o'clock positions on the steering wheel. I had done it! All the hard work had paid off. I felt like leaping in the air but contented myself with a simple smile.

Although taking a driver's test is commonplace, the manner by which I chose to do it is reflective of my gumption and a high degree of self-pride. It demonstrates my willingness to sacrifice easy for the sake of accomplishing what I deem to be of a higher worth (in this case, passing on a manual transmission).

Years later while a medical student, I conducted research in London and Uppsala, Sweden, and went traveling through Europe on weekends and again for three weeks after I finished my studies. I always traveled by myself. I felt free and independent, invigorated. Friends and colleagues strongly encouraged me to stay in hostels, arguing that they were safe and put me in touch with other American students. What they didn't understand is that I was intent on avoiding contact with other Americans: I wanted to immerse myself in the cultures of the places I ventured, to intermingle with their people, and communicate as best as I could regardless of the language barriers. I had purchased Arthur Frommer's, *Europe on 5 Dollars a day: A Guide to Inexpensive Travel*, which listed the names and phone numbers of Europeans who would house visitors in their homes for a relatively small fee. These were not bed and breakfasts; they were far less formal, more like visiting family. I loved the concept, and this was how I chose to travel.

So it was that I arrived at the train station in Munich and, using a public phone, called a home listed in Frommer's book. "Sprechen Sie Englisch?" I inquired. "Nein," was the host's reply.

"Zimmer, bitte?" I asked about the room. "Ja." I continued, "Wo ist hause?" Using my suspect German and patience on both of our parts, I obtained what I thought were directions to her house by way of the bus.

I soon discovered however, that my German was worse than I'd thought. When I exited the bus I walked in all directions in search of the street she'd mentioned, to no avail. A gentleman stopped and pointed down one street towards a "hostel." "Nein, bitte. Ich mochte hier gehen." I showed him the address. When he said, "Ach du lieber (good heavens)," I knew I was in trouble; yet I maintained complete confidence that I was intended to stay at the planned location.

A woman joined our conversation, and conferred with the man in writing bus and street directions for me. When the bus arrived, she explained to the driver where I needed to exit. "Vielen dank fur Hilfe," I thanked the woman for her help. "Bitte schon," she replied.

Shortly thereafter I was greeted by a short, stocky, ruddy-faced woman of about sixty, at a three-bedroom house with an eclectic mix of furnishings—antique Queen Anne sofa in the living room, yellow tile floor and frilly curtains in the kitchen, a heavy, four-poster oak bed and matching dresser in my room.

After settling in, I went out for a walk around the neighborhood. The homes were small, but their yards were well-maintained and abundant with flowers. Two blocks away, in a lovely park shaded by oak trees, children played tag and rode the swings. I ate spatzle and bratwurst at a charming little restaurant, and played a game of seeing how many words I recognized in the overheard conversations of my fellow diners.

When I arrived back at the house, the Hausfrau was eager to show off a picture album of her family—a daughter, slender with sharp cheekbones, herself mother to two small children; a dark-haired and muscular son and his wife; and a balding, stocky man with a wide grin. Tears welled in her eyes. "Toten," she murmured, "drei monaten." I put my hand on top of hers and told her I was sorry. "Danke," she whispered. Yes, my intuition was right, I was meant to stay at this specific place.

I was compelled to visit the Dachau concentration camp. I spent an entire day there, reading the stories of some of the two hundred thousand prisoners, crying at pictures of the emaciated and sick, nauseated by the images of corpses strewn on the grounds or piled high. I stood for a long time in the crematorium, running my hand over the pictures and names on the wall. I was especially appalled by the "medical" experiments of Dr. Sigmund Rascher, who tested how long prisoners could be immersed in cold or scalding water before they succumbed. I flinched at the imagined screams and unbearable pain to which these people were subjected. I'm not Jewish, but my mother's parents came over from Germany (her maiden name was Heidegger), and I wondered if, had I been there, I'd have had the courage to stand up to such a horror.

That evening I brought a bouquet of purple, white and yellow flowers back to the house. The Frau placed them in a vase and set them on her dining table. When I left the next morning we shared a heartfelt "Vielen Dank." I was happy that I'd not gone to a hostel.

Several days later, in Oslo, Norway, I was awestruck at the sight of Thor Heyerdahl's original Kon-Tiki. I had been enthralled and captivated by his book about the balsa wood craft, in which he and five crew members sailed from Peru to Tahiti in 1947, proving Heyerdahl's theory that ancient South Americans could have settled the South Sea Islands in such boats. The Kon-Tiki comprised only materials available in pre-Columbian times; Heyerdahl used no metal in building the boat. The scientific community had dubbed him a fool, suicidal, but after 101 days at sea, Heyerdahl and company smashed into a reef at Raroia in the Tuamotu Islands, 4,300 miles from their journey's start in Peru.

I admired his tenacity and the strength of his beliefs. He knew that the expedition was the only way to test his hypothesis, and he would not be deterred by the doubts of others. I wanted that same strength of conviction. As I stood before the Kon-Tiki I was filled with a resolve to emulate Heyerdahl, should I ever be tested. As it turned out, Alyona and Alec made voyage on the Kon-Tiki seem a cake-walk.

In the early eighties, six years after becoming health director in a rural part of my state, I began to worry that I had lost some of my clinical skills and acumen. Although I devoured the medical literature to keep my professional knowledge current, my direct exposure to patients was limited. A health director's roles include environmental risk assessment, communicable disease investigation and exposure, and community education, but minimal participation in family planning and/or pediatric clinics. I decided to take a three-month educational leave and to function, without pay, as a first-year pediatric resident at Charity Hospital, affiliated with Tulane Medical School in New Orleans.

The faculty was in disbelief that as a board-certified pediatrician I would want to subject myself to the rigors, exhaustion and stress demanded at that training level. They offered alternatives: I could serve as a fellow under the tutelage of a renowned specialist, for instance. I was not to be dissuaded. I didn't want an academic experience; I truly believed that I had to re-experience the challenges of sleepless thirty-six hour hospital duty, complex diagnostic dilemmas, adrenalin-charged emergencies, and face-to-face contact with families in frightening and dire situations. There was no other way I could come to grips with my simmering self-doubt as a clinical physician.

I dived into this three-month experience. I elected to work on the Contagious Disease Ward during the winter months. Tired but focused, I relished the wee-hours call to the emergency room to work-up a child with fever and seizures. I pored over studies and textbooks detailing confusing cases, and tried to learn from the hospital's specialists. I sat with patients' families, and was enriched and grounded by their hope, by strength that overshadowed despair.

In the end, my self-confidence was renewed, my competence confirmed. And I'd come to see that public health was the right professional career for me. I had re-experienced the compulsion and drive that made every minute of every day revolve around the patients, their families and the hospital. I couldn't leave work at the office: I spent my few off hours constantly re-examining my cases, my actions. Invigorating as it had been, and as good for my patients, it was not a realistic way to live. This realization would not have come to me, I don't think, had I been willing to take the easier path of working directly with a faculty member rather than as a first-year resident. In retrospect, this introspection prompted a pivotal life-altering direction. Had I decided to return to a clinical, or practice type career, the intensity of my engagement would have precluded any future adoption considerations.

These experiences—the Studebaker driving test, the European travels, the repeat clinical sojourn—reflect core facets of my personality. I'm a person of strong determination and focus; one who will always choose right over easy. Challenges fuel my resolve and tenacity. I won't be deterred by naysayers or seemingly impenetrable barriers. I also don't like distance from the action; I need to touch it, smell it, feel its drama. I will take the rocky pathway because I believe that with hard work and persistence I can succeed and, by so doing, help make the world a better place. I have complete faith that I will find a solution when it's needed. I knew that parenting Alec and Alyona would be difficult, but I also knew that adopting them was the right thing to do. So I told myself over and over as our flight took us westward.

Alec discovered the earphones and music; Alyona, however, grew restless. She was angry that Alec preferred music to playing with her; she threw her own earphones to the floor and tried to do the same with his. I piled her lap with cookies, crackers and fruit, but she poured her soda onto the carpet and crushed the snacks, her actions calculated to bring attention. I noticed that when doing something wrong, she often stole a glance at me to gauge my reaction.

Laura found two vacant seats across the aisle, to which she and Alec escaped. He stood on his seat, rocking and singing to the music from his headphones, waving to passengers several rows away, shouting "Hello" and "America"—and, for no discernible reason, bursting with laughter every few minutes. Other passengers would clap to the rhythmic beat of his dancing. He was center stage and loving it. At one point I borrowed his headphones and was amazed to hear classical music. Alec was jamming to Beethoven!

Alyona, on the other hand, was making an excellent case for why flight attendants should receive hazardous duty pay. She refused to wear her seatbelt. Magazines, headphones, shoes and anything else she could grab became projectiles, much to the annoyance of the other passengers. I offered her stuffed animals as desperate bribes; at most, they bought ten minutes of quiet.

When we arrived at our layover in Amsterdam, two attendants commandeered an electric cart and escorted us to a VIP lounge with a playroom area. The room had new, thick carpeting and plush leather chairs. Coffee, snacks and sodas were free and limitless. Clocks indicating times in different parts of the world hung on one wall. "Good luck," said the attendants, looking a bit more haggard than when we'd started our flight. As they walked away, I overheard one say in a loud whisper, "In this case, the VIP lounge stands for 'Very Irritating Passengers.'"

The children instantly gravitated to the toys, and for a few minutes, an observer might have mistaken them for well-behaved siblings. Alec pushed cars and trucks on important assignments, adding motor and horn sounds along the way. Alyona dressed and redressed dolls.

But the peace ended when we announced that we'd have to leave the playroom to get on another plane. Laura and I "football" carried the children through the airport to the next gate. Crowds parted as people saw and heard us coming.

Passengers at the gate complained bitterly to the officials and to us about the pair's disruptive behavior: "Can't you control your kids?" one asked. "Give them to me and I'll get them to behave," another offered. "You have no right having kids if you can't handle them," a third said.

It was futile to try to explain. We couldn't spare the time, anyway: The children screamed and pulled our hair if we held them, and kicked people, suitcases and chairs if we didn't.

Everyone was an expert on child-rearing—"They need a good spanking, both mother __and__ children, I heard; and, "They should give medicine to the children to make them sleep"—but none offered us help. Finally, an airline official took us out of line and into a private room. I could feel the stares from the other passengers. A few gave not-so-subtle sighs as we passed. The official got our boarding passes, then escorted us onto the plane. We were again in the last row near the doors and the galley.

For nine hours Alec moved to the beat of his music, and Alyona just moved. She raced up the aisle grabbing passengers' magazines or children's toys, dodging me when I followed.

The flight attendants, inordinately patient, several times led Alyona to the galley where they entertained her by opening the cabinets and letting her explore the many drawers.

It only took a moment's turn away to lose her again, and once, she ran straight to the cabin's big rear door. "Nyet, nyet!" I shouted. I grabbed her just as she was preparing to pull down the lever to open it. Nothing would quell Alyona's screams at not being allowed to open the door. She wanted out and couldn't understand why we wouldn't let her leave. She could see nothing in the pitch-black beyond the windows; the engines' constant roar only added to her desire to move

Our fellow passengers were by now openly hostile, shouting, "Keep your child in your own seat," and "My kid's sitting still, why can't yours?" and "Why didn't you bring enough toys and things for her to do?" I never confessed to being a pediatrician for fear of giving the profession a bad name.

By the time we reached New York and had to go through customs, we had dwindling control of two overtired and over-stimulated children. Holding their hands sparked explosive and violent tantrums. Letting them run wild saw them shove and kick strangers on the escalators, grab toys from other children, and lift merchandise from the concourse shops. Laura and I had our hands full even without them, as we had two carts of luggage and four backpacks. I begged for a ride on a passing terminal cart. "Sorry," the skycap driving it said. "It's only for the handicapped or elderly."

Alyona screamed and kicked my leg. Alec bit Laura's arm as she kept him from running away. "Actually, we are a little handicapped," I told him.

He shook his head. "Only handicapped or elderly. I'm not going to lose my job because you can't handle your kids." I stared in disbelief as he drove off.

While waiting for our luggage, Laura and I sat on the floor constraining the children in pediatric holds. Laura's legs were firmly wrapped around Alec, his arms tightly crossed over his chest. I had the same lock on Alyona. Cracker crumbs, mixed with spittle, ringed us on the floor and clung to our shirts and shorts. All of our faces were flushed and our bodies moist with sweat. The conveyer belt noisily transported suitcases to waiting hands. We had no waiting hands, and watched helpless to claim them, hundreds of eyes on us, as our bags lumbered by twice.

Then, without warning, Laura shot to her feet and shouted, "These children have just been adopted from a Ukraine orphanage where they have spent their lives. They do not speak English and we do not speak Russian. We are not child abusers." She sat back down. The room was silent, save for the creaking of the luggage conveyer. Even the children were stilled—not, evidently, by what she'd said, as they couldn't understand it, but by her forcefulness. Stares from the crowd became furtive glances, and from that point on, when Laura spoke the children were more inclined to listen. The effect wore off about two hours later, but those were a blissful two hours.

They ended in spectacular fashion, when Alyona and Alec made a mad dash for the bathroom. I rushed after them, realizing once inside that it was the men's room. A tall man in a fine pinstriped suit stared at the wall over his urinal, pretending he was oblivious to the havoc at his back, but a squatty, balding man in a ruffled shirt that looked like he had slept in it for days waved his fist at us, screaming, "What the fuck are you doing here? Get the hell out."

Alyona was already in a stall with her pants down. Mumbling an embarrassed apology to the two men, I grabbed Alec and squeezed with him into Alyona's stall. When she was done, I announced our intent to leave. No one responded, so I bundled the three of us towards the exit. The kids thought it was great fun.

The final leg of the flight home was comparatively quiet. Alec's small, frail body was curled cat-like in my lap. Alyona slept with her head on my shoulder. Laura was silhouetted against the window, eyes closed. The hum of the plane's engine, the shadowy movements of other passengers and the mellow early morning light outside the window lulled me near slumber, and into a place of quiet faith. A place with no maps. A place where I hoped to find what I hadn't known I was seeking.

⌒

Touchdown, August 30, 1999: No guns, no military. As the plane's tires bounced hard on the tarmac I felt tension and anxiety lift away. It might prove an illusion, but it was comforting to be home—to speak the language, know the resources. I was not at the mercy of an interpreter; theoretically, I could exercise more control over the children. I was surrounded by people who knew and cared about me, and who'd be confident of my parenting skills. I knew that helping these children heal and become part of a loving, caring family would be a challenge far surpassing anything I'd faced as a doctor. It would take those friends and their encouragement, any wisdom imparted to me by my mother, and most of all my own belief in myself and the children, regardless of naysayers. I'd have to be resilient. I'd have to be tireless, physically and mentally. I'd have to be unafraid to ask for help. I'd have to be totally committed. I said a silent prayer for wisdom, patience, compassion, humility.

Pat, a chaplain and long time friend who is always encouraging, waited at the gate with a beautiful bouquet of flowers and a welcoming hug. Laura's fatigue faded when she saw her husband, Greg. She dashed into his arms. "I never realized how much I loved you," she told him. She was close to tears.

We had made it home. Laura had been right—no way could I have brought these children back by myself. She had indeed been a gift. Now the real work would begin.

Chapter 7

For several days we lived under a self-imposed lockdown. Back in Ukraine, I had e-mailed Pat to ask that she install locks high on the inside of all of my house's entry doors. I also asked that she stock the refrigerator and the pantry with enough food for a week. She'd done it, taking the additional smart step of picking up my stereo and computer, as well as anything that looked fragile. I was equipped to hunker down with Alyona and Alec, without outside interference. I felt like a scientist designing a laboratory observation of wild mice: I wanted to see how they'd interact with each other and with me when no other influence was present, no opportunity to play one adult against another. I wanted to see if I could glean insight into their personalities just by observing them. I wanted it understood that this family was them and me; that we were inseparable, that no matter what, we were in this together. Of course, they'd have to stay put; I couldn't have them getting outside and taking off. Otherwise, I'd have few rules during the lock-down other than not permitting harm.

Alyona took Alec by the hand and escorted him through my modest, three-bedroom house, playing the tour guide, talking incessantly. They jumped on all three beds to see who could bounce higher and made a game out of leaping for the ceiling fans' pull chains. They stuck their heads in my fireplace to peer up the chimney, emerging with ash and soot in their faces and hair. She showed Alec that she could leap down several steps at once and urged him to try it. She encouraged him to climb over the stair railing on the second floor and drop onto the landing. My first observation: Alec never questioned her leadership, and was eager to applaud Alyona's successes. Alyona, on the other hand, was not a gracious loser; rather than applaud Alec if he jumped farther, she insisted that they keep doing it until she beat him.

Over the course of the next several days, Alyona took all of the heels out of my closet and tried on each as she primped and preened in front of my mirrored closet doors. She would look at herself face-on, turn sideways, place her hands on her hips, hold her head with a slight tilt to the side. She grinned broadly at her image. She proved good with make-up, carefully limiting lipstick to her full lips. She also demonstrated a knack for finding things. If Alec lost a toy he would go to Alyona and she invariably pinpointed it.

I noticed, too, that she was uncomfortable with change. She didn't like variations in our routine. No one could sit in her chair in the living room or her seat at the table. When she was tired of watching a movie, she demanded that the TV be turned off; if she didn't get her way, she'd scream. She would choose the times she played with Alec, ignoring his requests to play if she wanted to do something else. Alyona's behaviors were harsh and sharp. I would cup her hand in mine and softly stroke her cheek saying, "Gentle, gentle"; hoping she could understand a softer touch.

Alec, awed by the trucks, cars and building blocks in his room, was content to play by himself for hours. When he couldn't sit still, he would tear through the house, flipping all of the light switches, flushing the toilets, struggling to open windows that were bolted shut. He loved to put towels or blankets on his head, stretching his mouth wide with his fingers, and parade with high steps before me, angling for a laugh. Once, he grabbed me by the hand and led me upstairs to the room above the garage. It's a finished, carpeted space with a large built-in desk, a sofa-bed and a sewing table with a portable sewing machine on top. He'd discovered that I kept thread and needles in one of the drawers. When we arrived upstairs, with exaggerated flair, he waved his arm towards the room and beamed broadly at his masterpiece. Using all ten spools, he had strung thread between both desks and the sofa, around both desk chairs, and crisscrossing the floor. Fine strands of white, yellow, blue, black, tan and green made a web of the whole room. My first impulse was to groan at the mess, but I glanced down at Alec, saw his still wide grin and sparkling eyes, his evident joy at his accomplishment, and mustered my brightest smile. He wrapped his scrawny arms around my legs and hugged.

My other observations were that Alyona was a risk-taker, astutely observant, creative. Alec was a follower, an inveterate clown, and the quintessence of curiosity. We survived the first few days with fewer explosions than those in Ukraine. We grew more accustomed to each other. Although not a realistic approach to child-rearing for the long haul, the absence of rules offered us a chance to start over, and to recover somewhat from the nightmare in Kiev. I needed the time to regain my confidence and to focus on the children. Soon I was ready to introduce Alyona and Alec to the neighborhood and a few of my friends. I invited people over for a casual pool party and cook-out.

On the day of the party, Alyona and Alec were excited to help me put down a plastic cover on the table, arrange paper plates, napkins and plastic utensils, and place drinks and cups on a side tray. They knew, without words, that something fun was about to happen. I felt like I was preparing for their coming-out party. I had specifically told guests not to bring toys or gifts as I was certain that the energy of a crowd eager to meet the children would be more than enough stimulation for them. As friends arrived, I realized how much I had missed adult conversation over the past week. And I welcomed having other adults engage the children while I simply sat and relaxed. I didn't even cook: Others brought side dishes and grilled the hot dogs and hamburgers. Alyona and Alec relished being the center of attention; they never lacked for someone to play with them.

Alyona loved being in the pool. Fearless, tireless, she jumped from the diving board, slid down the slide and emerged sputtering and laughing from an underwater dunking, unfazed by her inability to swim, even in water several feet over her head; she was always able to find a helping arm or back while splashing in the deep end.

Alec was content to stay in the shallows. He clung to whoever's arms were offered to him. He knew no strangers and responded to everyone with warmth and joy. Unlike Alyona, who sought the attention of everyone, he was happy with one-on-one contact. When Alec was on the screened porch and I waved and blew him a kiss from the pool, he immediately poked his hand through the screen, tearing an opening, in order to wave back. He seemed unaware that he'd done any harm. I chose to smile.

Our experiment continued. Together, we made the perfect indoor campsite. Four sofa cushions fit comfortably under two blankets draped over a chair to form a tent. The chief engineer, Alyona, told Alec what to do in Russian. My job, clear from the start, was to bring food and hold loose parts. For five days we ate breakfast, lunch and dinner in our tent. They devoured twelve bananas and twice as many cups of yogurt in 48 hours.

Outside it rained. Inside, we marched to loud pop rock, banging along on saucepans and spoons. Our parades always started and ended at the tent. Remnants of oranges, hot dogs, hard-boiled eggs, perogies, apples, bananas, cereal, ice cream and cookies turned up, crushed, between the pillows, under the sofa or caked in their hair.

Soon, the tent doubled to two rooms, the second devoted to the TV and endless Disney videos. Now all pillows in the house were arrayed on the living room floor. Alyona would dress up and prance throughout the house pointing to herself and say, "Princess." Alec attempted a version of "Whistle While you Work."

Another observation: I could see that Alec cringed in pain whenever he tried to eat anything but soup, yogurt or ice cream. Biting into anything of substance would prompt teeth to fall out of his mouth in pieces. Even when he wasn't eating, he would sometimes grasp his mouth and cry out as tears welled in his eyes.

This condition was the result of well-meaning visitors to the orphanage who doled out candy to the children, unmindful that they never brushed their teeth. It might as well have been shrapnel, for the effect it had. Among our first trips out of the house was to the dentist, who tried to make the necessary repairs over Alec's objections and struggles: In pain or not, the boy couldn't grasp the benefits of being stuck in the mouth with a needle then having a stranger bump around in there with strange pieces of metal.

We decided, eventually, that the dentist would make the repairs with Alec under general anesthesia at a local children's hospital. I scrubbed up as well, to walk him into the room. We made quite a pair, swishing down the hallway in paper booties and masks. The nurses were accustomed to working with children; they were kind, gentle and easy-going. Alec was given headphones and selected the music he wanted. Then I sat on the table holding him while he inhaled bubble-gum flavored anesthetic gas through a big mask. In a short while he was out. I kissed his forehead and retreated to the waiting room.

My friend Pat kept vigil with me as I gulped down coffee and paced. Now and then someone would stop by to update us on Alec's condition. Four hours after it began, the surgery finally ended, and I was able to visit him in the recovery room. Even while groggy and grimacing with pain, he insisted on singing.

The rain had a soothing effect. We sat for hours on the glider on the front porch watching the drops fall. The children would lie with their heads on my lap while I rocked back and forth. Lightning would elicit smiles and excited chatter. With thunder, their small bodies tensed, and they'd squeeze tightly against me.

When there was no lightning or thunder, they excitedly paraded outside. Rain was not a deterrent. They would simply continue the charades under umbrellas. They broke four umbrellas in one week.

And then, out of nowhere, it would happen: They would huddle, then charge me swinging sticks, shoes or portable phones, one attacking from the back, one from the front. The tent, the glider, the parades, Cinderella—it was all forgotten. They'd kick, bite and slug me. Perhaps one would grab a lamp and start swinging. When I grabbed for one child, the other would hit me in the back or bite my arm. If we were outside, they would throw dirt in my eyes. I was at a distinct disadvantage: I couldn't understand their shouts to each other. I'd use the lap restraining hold, but could only neutralize one attacker at a time; the unrestrained kid would yank fistfuls of hair from my head and kick me repeatedly in the ribs. If I bled, they'd become even more aggressive. It was as if they could smell it.

I had never witnessed such violence, especially from children. The adrenaline in me rose; I felt like striking out. I wanted to do whatever was required to get them to stop. These were not children; they were savages, and I was their prey. My anger just seemed to invigorate them. Their eyes sparkled when I grimaced in pain. There was no humanity in those eyes. There was no warmth.

They acted as if they expected me to physically harm them, and intended to inflict as much damage as they could before the inevitable payback occurred. When I shouted "Nyet, nyet" or repositioned my hold on the prone and struggling child, the free one would shield the captive's face, as if fending off a blow from me. It took every ounce of moral strength I had to keep from fulfilling their expectations. I knew I had the strength to halt the insanity, but also knew that violence begets violence—it could make them even crazier. We could be injured. It was a scary insight.

Our fights left me soaked with tears and sweat. The end was usually a function of endurance. They'd tire and, without warning, simply stop. The child on the floor would go limp and start tearlessly crying. The other one would turn on the TV, take my hand and invite me onto the sofa. They were confused that I was still upset. It was as if we all had just had a good workout.

At times, I'd be exhausted before they were, and would lug them upstairs to lock them into their bedrooms. I'd regain my composure while sitting in the hallway, listening to the ravings beyond the doors until they, too, tired. That only worked for a short while: They soon broke the locks.

They never showed remorse following an episode. They rarely seemed to need a reason for starting one; perhaps it was out of boredom, or some remnant of a Darwinian game at the orphanage. Perhaps they liked fighting or the rush of adrenaline. Perhaps they were immensely frightened by losing all that was familiar, pathetic though that was.

Of course, there was one type of outburst that was easy to predict—when they didn't get their way. A simple "No" would touch off the powder keg, though it was usually forgotten as the trouble escalated; the outburst became self-sustaining, fueled by its own fury. These fits happened every day, and often several times a day. The kids seemed to relish them. I was constantly tense and watchful, ready for the next outburst. Sensing my anticipation, they didn't disappoint.

Tantrums in the car or a store were the worst. I learned very quickly that I couldn't be concerned with what other people thought while I did what had to be done. When they erupted in a grocery store because I would not let them play catch with the apples, I immediately abandoned our shopping cart, tucked each child under my arm, and headed to the car. Heads turned, mouths opened and everyone got out of my way. I kept my eyes straight ahead, my mind focused.

I body pinned both of them against the car while I unlocked the door, then literally threw them in the back seat. They issued blood-curdling shrieks while kicking the seats, pulling my hair and hitting me in the face with their shoes. The car rocked. The windows fogged. When I could take no more abuse, I crawled into the back seat of my small Nissan and used wrestling holds I'd learned while growing up with two brothers.

Their bites brought blood on my arms and hands. Both Alyona and I got nosebleeds. It seemed a reasonable possibility that someone would call the police, and that I might be arrested for child abuse (our therapist's assurance that she'd intervene was not much comfort in the midst of the fight). Finally, however, their screams dwindled to whimpers, and they slumped in the seat, whipped. Part of me wanted to hug them and tell them it would be all right. Another part of me, the larger part, was too hurt, angry and drained. I settled for middle ground: I turned on the air conditioner, gave them bottles of water, and tried to calm my breathing.

As spent and bruised as I was after such episodes, I held fast to the belief that things would get better, that I'd be able to endure the physical punishment for however long it took them to heal. I was certain that we'd been brought together because we were right for each other spiritually, cosmically, organically. I also better understood how important it was for them to completely trust we would always stick together as a family, no matter the good or bad times. Only then could they feel safe to take charge of their behaviors. I prayed for patience. I only doubted whether I could answer their misbehavior in ways that would, in the end, help them: I had no benchmark or gauge to guide me; I had no way of knowing whether my responses to them were appropriate. I'd never even imagined behavior like theirs, and I was definitely intervening in ways not described or discussed during my education as a pediatrician.

I enrolled both children in half-day classes at the Quaker Friend's School. By default, I was semi-enrolled, too, because I attended with them. The staff was true to the school's mission to emphasize harmony and community, and on some days when the children's antagonism had me feeling battered and tense, walking onto the campus was like having a gentle hand on my shoulder, a balm to my spirit. Other days I cursed the cheeriness of the place.

The campus was a half-hour's drive from the house. We listened to loud, lively music and tried to spot "Baby Machinas", my Russo-English term for Volkswagen beetles. The trips became vocabulary-builders. I would name colors and point to items in the Nissan that matched. When jets from the nearby navy base zoomed overhead, the kids learned to point and shout, "plane." They were excited and eager to leave for "school," one of the first polite English words that they learned.

Alyona exhibited great creativity. She painted in bright colors and amazing detail. Her houses were outlined in red, boasted triangular roofs, and were ringed by colorful beds of flowers. Her trees had thick brown trunks and meticulously splotched leaves. At the top middle of every painting was a bright yellow sun, multiple rays spraying happy light.

At school, unlike at home, it was Alec who proved the bigger handful. He was exultant on the playground, playing with blocks, or pushing around a toy car or truck. But when items had to be put away or he was told to pipe down, that changed: Even the gentlest of the school's teachers provoked his rages, during which he'd hurl toys, kick, punch, scream, and bite.

We tried a time-out chair, rocking, walking. Alyona tried to calm him. Nothing worked, and his violent and disruptive behavior so frightened the other children that they started to avoid him. As he became more isolated, in not only language but social contact, his tantrums came more often, sometimes without a trigger. He must have been confused and hurt: Here was a boy who'd been the clown prince of the orphanage, who had compensated for being a malnourished runt by making the other children laugh, and now he was feared and shunned. Within a couple months, the school suggested that perhaps the children would do better in a public school.

Chapter 8

I grew up watching and playing baseball. I loved everything about the game: its sounds, its smells, its pace. My introduction came courtesy of my older brother, Eddie, who was his Little League team's first baseman and dominant slugger, and who for four years was a spring training batboy at Orlando's Tinker Field, first for the visitors, and later for the "hometown" Washington Senators. Mom and I went to every game. On the way home, Eddie would regale us with stories about the players he'd met. While he was in the locker room one day with the Brooklyn Dodgers, Jackie Robinson, Roy Campanella, Don Newcombe and Joe Black asked Eddie to fetch them lunch, and gave him enough money to get something for himself. When he returned, they invited him to eat lunch with them.

His favorite player was Frank "Spec" Shea, a pitcher for the Senators who'd sometimes ask Eddie to "catch me up"—to play catcher while Spec threw warm-up pitches. The sting of those pitches was trumped by Eddie's excitement and pride.

One afternoon, when the Senators were playing Detroit, Eddie ran out from the dugout to retrieve the bat, so that it wouldn't interfere with a coming play at home. As he did, the umpire grabbed the bat and, without looking, tossed it behind him. We could hear it thud against Eddie's head from four rows into the bleachers. Mom dashed to the car while I walked Eddie out of the stadium, one arm on his back and the other steering him into the parking lot. It might have been my first experience as a medical practitioner.

Eddie got five stitches at the emergency room and insisted on returning to the game. Mom dropped him off at the clubhouse. From the bleachers, we saw Eddie step onto the field, a huge gauze bandage wrapped around his head, and slowly walk the third-base line towards the dugout. The crowd roared and jumped to its feet.

Eventually I played the game myself. Orlando hosted an American Softball Association amateur women's fast-pitch softball team called the Orlando Rebels. At my insistence, my parents and I went to all Rebels' home games, and we learned that the team sponsored a girl's squad called the Little Rebels. I tried out for the team and made it.

Our coaches were the big Rebels' pitcher and catcher. I was rapt at their every word. I listened intently to their fielding and batting advice. I arrived early to each practice session. As I bent at the knees in ready position at second base, glove poised to catch the ball, I dared the batter to hit it to me. The exhilaration of a quick second base tag and a fast toss to first for a double play was almost boundless. I was not a strong batter, but I was fast, so I often surprised our opponents with a bunt and made it safely to first. Those were two of the most exciting years of my life.

I wanted Alyona and Alec to share my passion and love of baseball. I saw it as a key component of the American experience, a tool to help them assimilate, to acquire the trappings, the accent, of their new lives— and not least, to have fun. So I enrolled them on a Little League team. They still spoke very little English. To my knowledge, they had never seen baseball played. But I knew some of the team parents and trusted that they'd be kind.

I turned out to be right about them and, more importantly, the other kids on the team. Alyona and Alec were loved and accepted. They'd stand on home plate facing the wrong way. They'd swing before the ball was even thrown. Even the opposing teams grasped the situation; not once did they tease or yell at these strange little foreigners. This alone seemed a wonderful, unexpected gift. Alyona and Alec thrived on the attention they earned and on being part of a group.

Their hits, one each, came in the season's final two games. Both were slow-moving grounders. And their responses were the same: As the ball rolled towards the pitcher, each stopped dead, turned and gave me a huge grin. I was jumping up and down, screaming and pointing to first base. Each carefully placed the bat on the ground and ran straight for the ball. The coach dashed onto the field, turned each toward first base and ran beside them to make sure he or she got there. Both were thrown out, of course, but neither was the least bit disappointed. They'd made contact. They'd hit the ball.

Off the field, their team spirit wasn't nearly so impressive. A frequent source of conflict: seat belts.

Either because they didn't get what they wanted or were just tired of wearing them, the kids would unfasten their seat belts and stare at me from the back seat, defiant. I always answered the challenge the same way: I pulled the car to the shoulder, turned off the air conditioner, locked the doors and windows and waited; we would cook until the seat belt was clasped. I'd close my eyes and take long, slow breaths in an effort to slow my metabolism. I'd ignore the shouts and thumps in the back seat. The temperature soared. Salty sweat would cascade down my forehead, burning my eyes; my shirt would paste itself to my back. The children grew even wilder. They kicked and hit the seats. They screamed in half-English, half-Russian. Alec would strip off his shirt and wipe himself down with it.

Alyona was almost always the first to surrender. She'd snap her seatbelt closed, pleading with Alec to do the same. I'd watch in the rear-view mirror as Alyona's pleas turned into whines. Alec would sit with arms crossed over his narrow chest, his jaw clenched, lips pressed into a tight seal. He'd push her away if she reached for his seatbelt.

So we'd sit some more. Condensation dripped from the windows. Alyona sobbed. I reclined my seat and settled in for a long, hot wait. Alec's record was forty-two minutes.

Afterwards, we'd guzzle the bottled water I kept in the car. I figured the ritual, like dog obedience training, would eventually yield dividends; consistency was essential. So it did—after six such episodes, Alec finally concluded that fastening his seatbelt was far easier than enduring the sweatbox.

Trying another unconventional method to quell Alyona's and Alec's outbursts, I hung a fifty-pound, poly canvas heavy boxing bag from the garage rafters. The bag was "designed to withstand abuse," according to its label. Its manufacturer had not met my children.

Not long after the installation I dragged a kicking and screaming Alyona to the garage and planted her in front of the bag while I demonstrated two hard rights and then a left to its middle. "Arrrrgh," I grunted with each punch.

"Fuck you," Alyona responded.

So, bobbing her head butts, I grabbed her from behind and tied red training gloves onto each of her hands. When I released her, she swung at me hard, landing a solid blow to my mid-section, and for a moment I doubted the wisdom of the experiment. "I hate you, I hate you," she repeatedly yelled.

I snatched her by the wrists. "Hit it, Alyona, hit it," I yelled. I pulled her right arm back and slammed it hard against the bag. I slipped behind the bag, leaning against it with my left shoulder. "Now, Alyona, hit it."

She tapped at the bag with her right fist. Head bowed, she mumbled, "Go fuck, I don't want to do this."

I moved beside her, raised my right leg and kicked the bag with all my might. "Take that," I shouted. The bag swung sharply backward, then back, right at Alyona. I stepped in front of her, stopping the bag with a thud to my chest. Air exploded from my mouth. "Ha, ha," Alyona chortled, "I hope it hurt."

That ticked me off. I leaned in close, nose to nose with her, my jaw muscles tight and sweat dripping from my chin. "Hit the stupid bag. It's better than hitting me," I bellowed. "We're staying out here until you hit the stupid bag, I don't care how long it takes." Spittle sprayed her cheek.

I returned to my position, feet planted solidly on the concrete floor, bracing my left shoulder against the bag. "Do it, Alyona, do it." The original cause of her outburst had long since faded; my stubbornness was due less to my belief in the therapeutic effects of boxing than to my need to have her listen to me, and to redirect her venom to something besides me, if only briefly. Looking back, my screams, though harsh, sounded more like pleas than orders. For some reason, though, she didn't try to run back into the house. The novelty of my demanding that she actually hit this strange hanging object may have also been enough to hold her interest.

My sweat stained the canvas, and I half-whispered, "Please, Alyona, hit the stupid bag." I wanted this questionable experiment to end, but I didn't want to be the one to walk away from it.

Without warning, she issued a powerful right punch to the bag and then an immediate left. The bag swung into my shoulder, jolting me back to reality. "Yes, yes," I urged her on. She raised her right leg to kick and I tightened my leg muscles preparing for the impact. It was a ferocious kick, almost sending me to the floor, and accompanied by a stream of vitriol: "Take that, and that," and "You motherfucker." She delivered non-stop punches and kicks for fifteen minutes. Sweat glistened from her arms and dripped to the floor from her chin. Spittle sprayed the bag. My shoulder and legs burned.

As suddenly as she had launched the onslaught, she stopped, whimpering, arms limp by her sides. I pulled her close, stroked her matted hair. "It's all right, Alyona, it's all right," I reassured her. "You did good."

Over the next three months, both Alyona and Alec could often be persuaded to hit the bag instead of me or the contents of the house. They attacked it with unrestrained ferocity, twice ripping its canvas skin. The duct-tape repairs gave it character and fueled jokes during calm times. Eventually, though, the novelty of this outlet wore off, and they returned to their tried-and-true habits.

On those difficult mornings when struggles occurred and that dark, foreboding cloud encompassed us on our ride to school, I'd try to lighten the mood by yelling, "Gooood morning, world! I'm ready for you!" I'd wait for a response. Pouting, angry, they'd mumble unintelligibly...

They were no match for their persistent mom. I'd yell the phrase again, and again, and again—as many times, in as many different accents and intonations, as it took to get a rise out of them. Finally, perhaps just to shut me up, they'd join in. I viewed our battle cry as an act of solidarity. United, we confronted the world.

Each evening, as I tucked my weary or excited or frightened or hostile children into bed, I would remind them and me: "No matter how bad things may be, you are never going back to the orphanage." We were family, I'd say, and families stuck together in thick and thin. I loved them. I'd never leave them. They probably understood just a word or two, but I hoped that my gentle tone and expression gave them the message that they were safe. In time, as they picked up English, I knew that they'd come to understand me—and perhaps they would also have the memory of having heard these words from the very beginning of our time together.

For all of our rituals, for all of the happy moments we shared, however, parenthood was largely combat. The bad times, the blow-ups, were so extreme that they all but blotted out the good. Within six weeks of arriving in the States, I realized I needed help, and started therapy for the children using an interpreter. Our weekly visits often found me dazed from sleepless nights and trauma-filled days with the children. I couldn't help falling to sleep during some of the sessions; it was a welcome spell of calm.

I chose the therapist carefully. Patsy was in her mid-sixties, keenly observant, and had extensive experience with international adoptions. She'd helped patients with extreme issues who had been committed to institutions, and others who'd made great strides in outpatient therapy. You could not intimidate or manipulate Patsy; her voice might be soft and soothing but she demanded respect and compliance.

She educated me about "oppositional defiance," the clinical term for the free-for-all the children launched against me. She helped me understand that it was rooted in fear, anxiety, shame and an absence of trust, rather than any true hostility. It also signaled their expectation that I, like everyone else who'd come and gone in their lives, would reach my limit and give up on them, so they might as well keep pushing my buttons and spur the inevitable. Emotionally, the children were paralyzed at less than two years of age. In order to change behaviors, they first had to learn to trust me—-to trust that no matter what happened I would always be there for them.

Patsy also helped me to understand that the children perceived expressions of love as vulnerability, as weaknesses to be exploited. They had no concept of love from the heart; it was simply words, a lowering of defenses that could be used to their advantage. They also had no understanding of emotions in general and how to read facial expressions. I put emoticons on the refrigerator and pointed to the appropriate face representing what one of us might be feeling—-anger, frustration, happy, sad.

Although Alyona had repressed most of her memories of abandonment and of her time on the street, some of her behavior was classic for abused children. She would defecate on the floor or in her underclothes. Sometimes, she smeared the mess on the walls and herself. She rocked constantly, back and forth, back and forth. At home or in Patsy's office, she was in motion.

Alec rocked too, though in his case, Patsy suspected that his history of emotional deprivation had left him so numb that he was driven to seek feeling. His rocking thus was violent: He swung from side to side with such force that his bed would shake and he'd bruise himself. It was frightening to watch.

Another leftover of their orphanage days: The children stashed food in nooks throughout the house. They comforted them, these caches. They recalled their past hunger pangs, and sought to protect themselves against that pain's return.

Through the interpreter I made contact with two Ukrainian women who agreed to watch the children and help teach them English. Frieda was short and stocky with a quiet, almost timid manner. Her demeanor announced her eagerness to please. It was quickly ruptured by the children. Her gentleness made her an easy target.

As long as few demands were placed on them, Alyona and Alec were playful, compliant and enjoyed themselves. But as I knew too well, they could switch in an instant to intimidating, and Frieda, grandmotherly prey that she was, had no defense, physical or emotional, in those moments. Once, Alyona grabbed the steering wheel of the car while Frieda drove. Alec often buried her under an avalanche of profanity. Frieda reported these offenses with woeful commiseration. "I'll pray for you," she said. And: "God will bless you in Heaven." And: "Alec is the devil and a very bad boy." She lasted about two months. "I don't feel safe," she explained. "I don't want anyone to get hurt." I understood completely.

The second Ukrainian sitter was younger, in her early forties. I had hopes for her: She walked with a strong, almost martial, stride, harbored concrete opinions, wasn't too polite or timid to avoid interrupting any conversation.

But teaching English to the children masked her covert agenda: She was a Ukrainian patriot who adamantly opposed foreign adoptions. I arrived home one day to piercing, fearful stares from the children as the sitter spoke forcefully to them, occasionally pounding her fists. She did not acknowledge my arrival or answer my question about what she was saying. Finally, I recognized some words and their meaning—abuse, America and bad. "I don't think I like what you are saying to them," I told her. "I would like you to leave."

She kept talking without a glance my way. I put my hand firmly on her elbow and almost lifted her out of the chair, saying: "Please leave."

She spun toward me and, shaking a finger in my face, shouted, "You have no right to take these children out of their home country. You are abusing them by keeping them here in America. This is child abuse." The kids watched, transfixed. "I told them you are trying to control them and make them American," she sputtered. "It is a plot to destroy Ukraine. You need to take them back to Ukraine or they need to leave now!"

I was stunned. And some kind of ticked off. "You must leave now," I told her, struggling to keep my tone even. "You are no longer welcome in my home. You have no right to speak to my children this way."

She stood fast. I grabbed her elbow and escorted her to the door, pushed her outside, and shut it behind her. She was still yelling.

I stood with my back to the door, gulping air. I had never been so assaulted for doing what I'd thought was right. Worse, though, was that she'd launched the attack in front of the children, who now looked at me with anger and suspicion. They rejected hugs or any signs of tenderness that evening. They did not want to be in the same room with me. They tried to flee. Eventually, the house was beset by a grand mal outburst that went on for hours, until they finally dropped from exhaustion. Property damage was significant.

I then had a tag-team of young sitters—a local high school senior and a recent college graduate, in both of whom the children met their match in endurance and determination. Michelle and Annie had the physical courage to be unintimidated by Alyona and Alec. They were flexible, intelligent and mentally prepared for pretty much anything the kids might try.

Annie, an expert outdoorswoman, was intrigued by the pair's bizarre and unpredictable behavior. She researched international adoptions and oppositional defiance, and brought scholarly articles and studies for us to discuss, so that we might develop new strategies for dealing with them. Michelle, the younger, served as disciplinarian, and enforced the boundaries. Both girls were even-tempered, icy-cool, even. Neither could be goaded by Alyona's and Alec's assaults, even when they were suffering cuts, bruises and abrasions.

The children went on day trips with Michelle's family, and Annie's family beach cottage became their weekend haunt; they spent hours collecting shells there and showing off their treasures. Annie's mother, Mary Pehlam, adopted me as well as the kids, volunteering to watch the children and take them to school when I had professional conflicts. On one occasion she called the house and the children told her, "Mom sick. In bed." Within an hour, Mary Pehlam arrived at the house, grocery bag in hand, to prepare dinner for the children, pack all of our bags and tote us to her house, where she mothered us for three days.

The beach itself was therapeutic for the children, though not in the way it is for most of us. It tended to be crowded with people and activity, which they seemed to crave. The children didn't seem to trust calm; perhaps, I realized, they were even afraid of it.

Bustle seemed an addiction for which they required a periodic "fix." I came to understand that it was a byproduct of life in the orphanage. Extended calm seemed mute, lifeless.

On Thanksgiving Mary Pehlam went to great trouble preparing a Ukrainian feast and to decorate the table in the country's style. She cooked dishes using a Ukrainian cookbook she'd found at the library. There were lots of potatoes and cabbage. Annie and her brother, Richard, had come back home for the occasion.

In spite of our admonishments, Alec insisted on trying to climb on the family's golden retriever. The dog was a gentle animal but had diseased hips, and kept trying to escape. While all adults were looking elsewhere, Alec tried one time too many.

We heard screams and snarls. Mary Pehlam got to Alec first, and rushed towards me holding a screaming, bloody mess. The mom in me cowered but the doctor took charge. "To the kitchen table," I ordered. "Lights and towels."

The kitchen became an emergency room. Lewis, Mary Pehlam's husband, cleared the table. Alec had deep cuts under one eye, on his left cheek, and his forehead. His upper lip was split on both sides. Blood gushed from every laceration. I was relieved to see that his eyes were untouched, however, and he'd suffered no arterial bleeds.

Alec whimpered that he didn't want to go to the hospital. Mary Pehlam was near tears.

When we got the bleeding stopped, the mom in me returned to the fore. My legs turned weak. I wobbled to the car and sat in the back seat with my arms outstretched to receive Alec. Gently, as if handing me a newborn baby, Mary Pehlam's husband placed the sniffling Alec on my lap. I held him close as we were driven to the emergency room.

Forty stitches later, Alec emerged with a swollen, bruised face. He was wiser for the experience. "I hurt dog, Mommy," he said of it a few days later. "I sorry."

⤸

Public school was a godsend. Our city's district had the resources, experience and patience for special-needs children. Alyona learned English quickly, and soon enjoyed sharing a book on Odessa with her classmates. She had sharp powers of observation and a good sense of when to keep to herself or when she might be able to distract without getting into trouble. But an important core of her personality was a sincere love of learning—both by observation and by listening.

She reveled in the attention that came with being different. Not infrequently, playground activities became a competition for her to take charge—a remnant from her years at the orphanage. The other children, captivated, tolerated her quirks. Her kindergarten teacher, Mrs. Arseneau, used a gentle touch on the shoulder or a hug to appropriately redirect Alyona. Alyona rarely resisted. Best of all, she was able to stay on task academically.

But she had a dark side. At home she would stand at her open bedroom window and shout obscenities at the neighborhood children. "You fuck." "You bitch." "Go to hell."

When she didn't get her way, she continued to throw violent tantrums. She was violent and wantonly destructive: Strong beyond her years, she kicked holes in walls and hurled anything she could put her hands on. Her aim improved all the time.

Alec, on the other hand, was frightened by school. While Alyona strode smartly to class, Alec backed away; he sometimes led his teachers on a chase through the cafeteria to avoid being corralled. No amount of cajoling reassured him. Most mornings, I would carry him kicking, screaming, hair-pulling and head butting to his desk.

His fellow students and his teacher, Mrs. Snydor, were saints. Their morning ritual was to immediately gather around this sobbing, combative child with calm voices and friendly puppets. Their concern penetrated deep into his fearful spirit. They did what children do best—enveloped him with their hearts.

"Don't be afraid," said the brave, golden-maned lion.

"Let's play," said the gangly-armed monkey.

"I like you," said the jumping dolphin.

But it was the big, soft, cuddly brown bear that had the greatest success changing tears to smiles. "I'll protect you," said the bear. And Alec would hold him close.

Throughout the school day, Mrs. Snydor was undaunted by his regressive episodes of confrontation. She was tall, self-assured, and was able to calmly maintain order while confronting Alec's near-panic.

On occasion, when I would make a surprise visit to his classroom, I would find Mrs. Snydor on the floor with one arm wrapped around a struggling Alec and her legs wrapped firmly but gently around his legs. Her other hand held the book she was reading to all the children sitting attentively on the floor, mesmerized by her animation and ability to bring the book to life. Not understanding the language, Alec was oblivious to the pleasures of the story.

His frustration at limited communication was manifested in physical outbursts. Not unlike an infant or early toddler, he would scream, point or throw things when he wasn't getting what he wanted. His delayed development hampered his creative abilities to mime, draw or otherwise express his wishes and needs. In a fit of exasperation and adrenaline he pulled down a six-shelved book-case, sending books, papers and knickknacks spilling onto the classroom floor. Fortunately, no one was hurt. My heart ached at seeing such a loving, gleeful child imprisoned by his rage and exasperation. America had little to recommend it to someone who didn't understand what was happening around him. That said, Alec was like an excited two-year-old when presented with new toys, picture books and classroom games. He reveled in any activity set to music. He danced, he rocked, he sang. He "shared" his experiences with ballads of amalgamated English/Russian words set to his own odd musical rhythms.

At home, he preferred to stick close to Alyona, feeling secure with a compatriot who spoke the same language. He tended to mirror her: When Alyona was calm, Alec was good-humored and light-hearted. When she was sullen, or rude, or violent, he'd join her. Sometimes, it seemed that she enjoyed the power she held over him: With an evil glint in her eye, she'd start an argument with me, spur Alec to a craze of combative energy, then fade into the background. Alec would be unable to dial down his aggression; Alyona would sit back and watch the show.

All this conflict took its toll on Alec. "Alec was a little distant today," my son's teacher, Ms. Gwaltney said. "He said that Alyona got angry last night and he was afraid that she would hurt you or him."

"Yes, she had a meltdown last night," I responded. "It wasn't very pretty."

"I want you to know that I'm required by law to report this to the Child Protection Services," she said.

I was speechless. A swirl of thoughts and fears swept through my head: What if this gets in the newspaper? What will people think of me? I often work with Social Services; this will be very awkward. How could anyone think I'd hurt, or let anyone hurt, Alec or Alyona? Why didn't Alec just tell me? Will this affect my job? I expressed none of these fears. I simply said, "OK. I understand that you were doing your job."

My gut reaction was to be upset at Alec. I even contemplated calling Social Services to see if the investigation could be avoided. Instead, I decided to not subject Alec to any of my concerns but rather hear what he had to say.

"Your teacher called today," I said, by way of broaching the subject. "She said you were worried about what Alyona might do when she's angry."

"I am, Mommy," he said. "She scares me when she's mad. I'm afraid that she'll hurt us."

I realized that my concerns had all related to me, and my desire to protect me from adverse publicity or public shame. Not once had I looked at the real issue.

I wrapped my arms around him, "I'm sorry she scares you," I told him. "We'll work it out."

In order to avoid conflict of interest, the case was referred to a social services office in a neighboring city. Its case workers came to my home for the interview. Although they were professional and non-judgmental, I still felt like a child who had been sent to the principal's office for cheating. They asked probing questions: What do you do when Alyona has a meltdown? How do you protect the children from getting hurt doing the episode? Is your family receiving therapy? Have you ever hit the children? Do you have someone to help you when you're at your wit's end? I didn't have good answers for a lot of the questions.

"I just do the best I can at the time," I meekly replied to a few of the inquiries. "I love my children. I would never do anything to hurt them."

They spoke with teachers and the children, and researched my background for any whiff of a criminal bent. It was a humbling and deflating experience. I perceived that my parenting skills were under the spotlight; it took a great deal of effort on my part, and reassurance from them, for me to maintain the focus and perspective that this was not about me, but about helping Alec feel safe in his own home. They offered constructive suggestions for Alec during times of stress: Stay in his room or go to a neighbor's house. They emphasized to both children that I would do everything possible to protect them. It was a valuable reminder to keep the children, not me, at the forefront, and that lesson stayed with me throughout some of the most difficult times.

Though I didn't realize it, being a pediatrician might have been a disadvantage in those unsteady days. Perhaps not having birthed Alyona and Alec was, too. Whatever: It took one of the secretaries at work to push me from a "family in study" to just plain "family." I was talking with Terri about the shenanigans of "the boy" and the obstinate defiance of "the girl." Herself a parent, she listened sympathetically. Then, with both kindness and wisdom, she said, "Dr. Welch, these children are not 'the boy' and 'the girl.' They are your children, not patients. They are your son and daughter, and you are their mother."

The words had a powerful impact on me. I was unable to speak as they sunk in. I couldn't even <u>say</u> the words <u>son</u> and <u>daughter</u>. I walked away in a daze, trying to digest the truth of it.

Chapter 9

It was our first spring, and we embarked on a day devoted to a key American rite of passage: bike-riding for the first time. Alyona's reluctance to admit any lack of skill, to display any weakness, proved a strong motivator for her to learn quickly. She refused my assistance. I took no offense; survival on the streets, I figured, had required bravado. Weakness invited abuse or harm. She had learned her lessons well.

Alec just enjoyed the bike's rolling speed, the wind in his face, even falling—that was part of the fun. He wasn't out to prove anything. His sociability complicated his progress at staying up: Why look forward while pedaling when he could turn to talk with me as I pushed him? After several impressive crashes, I had him push off from the curb and ride towards me as I ran backwards ahead of him.

The day's bright spirit changed come bedtime. After dinner both kids became hyperactive and excitable, running through the house and engaging in the fighting games common to the orphanage; sticks were swords and shoes, pencils, and videos were projectiles. At first, it was in fun. They screamed with delight when they could ambush me or each other. They plotted in Russian to elude me.

But soon they were wrestling each other, and it was no longer a game. They twisted each other's necks, pushed with mounting ferocity. Neither would listen to my orders to break it up. I'm not sure they even heard me.

Since Alec was lighter and easier to carry, I plucked him away and toted him off to his room, his arms and legs swinging wildly. They had broken the locks, so I had to hold his door shut, while Alyona kicked, hit and bit me. I stood firm, holding the knob and praying that I could last longer than she could.

Alec's room sounded like a battlefield. He was hitting and kicking the walls and door, throwing dresser drawers to the floor. I heard glass shatter—there went the mirror. Other sounds I couldn't identify, though they were certainly loud. I held the door handle with every bit of strength I could muster, bent on confining the destruction and rage to one room.

He screamed a stream of Russian and English expletives. I could sense the venom in his voice. The walls and door shook. Even Alyona grew unnerved, and quit her attacks on me; in fact, she retreated to her room and curled up with her hands over her ears. Alec had never acted like this.

I debated the value of letting the storm continue in his room, versus going in to calm it. I opted to stay out, and to keep alert to any sounds suggesting he had hurt himself. I was scared for our safety more than angry—scared, in part, because I didn't know what to do or whom to turn to. I could count on no physical or emotional relief, on this night or for the foreseeable future. My muscles ached and my hands were sweaty. Mostly, I feared that I wouldn't be able to hold the door closed, and that Alec would escape and hurt Alyona, himself or me. I was scared that I'd misread the sounds beyond the door, and that when I entered the room I'd find that he was seriously injured. My once well-ordered life had turned surreal.

During a brief interlude in Alec's fit, I called my friend Pat on my cell phone. She could hear the noise in the background. "I'm on my way," she said. "Hang in there."

Peace came before she arrived. Alec's curses became anguished sobbing; his kicks and punches came slower. The insanity had lasted for what seemed an eternity, but in reality had been about forty minutes. I opened the door to find him drenched in sweat, his skin bright red. His eyes were unfocused. His breathing was rapid and shallow. Crunching over broken glass, scaling an upended mattress and box spring, I moved toward him. Too numb and shell-shocked to even cry, I pulled him onto my lap as I assessed the damage. There were five holes in the walls, varying in size from two inches to seven or eight. Some had clearly been made with a fist or foot. A couple defied explanation until I spied a curtain rod on the floor. He'd used it to punch a big hole in the door, too.

Clothes were strewn all over the room and hanging from the ceiling fan's blades. The six-drawer dresser was tilted at a thirty-degree angle, two of its legs imbedded in the wall. The curtains were down. The Venetian blinds had been wrenched loose by the cords. And incredibly, the metal bed frame—solid steel—had been bent at a fifteen-degree angle.

Alyona tiptoed across the debris-strewn floor holding two glasses of water, saying, "This will help, Mommy." Her tone was contrite.

Pat arrived. She took several deep breaths as she strove to grasp the devastation. Pat, who comforts people with terminal illnesses for a living, used cold water, a light touch and gentle words to calm Alec, who was coming around and, with a dawning horror, beginning to recognize all he had done.

He had no memory of what had touched him off. He could not recall his destructive acts. It was as if he'd been through an exorcism.

Is this what it was like when you stepped onto a battleground after the firing stopped? I was in a disconnected, ethereal state, and, strangely, a place of profound divination. Amidst the havoc I felt spiritually calm.

For the first time, I felt I wasn't merely a caregiver: It was as if I had just experienced labor, and birthed two fragile lives who'd forever look to me for guardianship, unconditional love, hope and devotion. Out of chaos and destruction, I had somehow gained a sense of family. I had, for better or worse, for good times and bad, a son and daughter.

Following one meltdown or other, I decided it was important that the children know how to call 911 should we need immediate emergency assistance. They were quick to master the sequence on the phone's touch pad. I considered the lesson learned.

I was taking a shower one Saturday morning when Alyona rushed into the bathroom, crying: "Mommy, a policeman is in the house." Right. I kept washing. She insisted a cop was on the premises. When she wouldn't stop, I threw a bathrobe over my dripping skin and, leaving a trail of water behind me, followed Alyona into the hallway overlooking the stairs. At their foot stood a uniformed patrolman.

He spoke first: "Good morning, ma'am."

I managed a feeble hello.

My evident surprise and embarrassment prompted him to explain. "The children dialed 911, and when our return phone call was not answered, they sent me to check on the house," he said. "I asked them if an adult was in the house, and they said no, so I came in. Are these your children?"

Well, here was confirmation: The kids knew how to dial for help. "Yes," I said. "I just taught them how to dial 911." They hadn't lied to him, I added: We used the word grown-up, rather than adult. "They're recently from Ukraine so have limited English vocabulary," I told him. "I was in the shower and didn't hear the phone."

He lectured the children on when to use 911 as I stood statue-like in a growing puddle of water. Then he tipped his hat; I said goodbye, thanked him, and watched him go as the children chatted excitedly about the man with the gun. Alec and Alyona understood the thinking behind 911 a little better after that. A couple of years later, as it turned out, we'd come to depend on it.

Alec and Alyona had a profound effect wherever we went, but perhaps nowhere more memorably than the Episcopal Church I'd attended for years, where we ventured every Sunday morning for the eleven o'clock service. We always sat in a side section near an exit and invisible to the rest of the congregation. The families around us were accustomed to filtering out chatter and the sounds of play. They hadn't met the likes of us, however. Father John, our priest, was middle-aged and calm and focused on you when you spoke to him. The children took to him and his wife, who had a background in child development, and viewed Sunday mornings as an opportunity to socialize with them, and with other members of the congregation who had become a part of their lives. As Father John marched up the aisle in his white robe and colorful hassock, they waved and shouted hello to him. When receiving communion at the altar rail, they stood to hug him.

When Elaine, a friend and Alyona's godmother, walked to the altar with the choir, they dashed after her. When she stood to sing, the children cheered and waved. When Pat read from the scriptures, the children shouted excitedly, "Ms. Pat, Ms. Pat." And when cake was served for special occasions, they grabbed several slices.

Which is to say that those early days weren't all bad. Mixed in with the rages and tears, were some moments of hilarity. It's just that I never knew which I'd get.

Chapter 10

After ten months in the States, the children's English had improved substantially; however, they remained a little shaky in their understanding of some words. "Vacation," for example, could mean "Mom pointing to pictures in books," or "Mom talking excitedly," or "Mom buying us lots of snacks." They had never had a vacation, after all.

But it seemed time to introduce them to the concept. God knows, I needed a break. So I reserved a time-share in Cumberland County, Tennessee, mountain country laced with hiking trails, wooded gorges and waterfalls. Our ten-hour drive would be rewarded with serenity, or so I imagined. Talia, a high school student, had bravely agreed to go with us. She was a quiet, reserved young lady who was a voracious reader. She approached life at an easygoing stroll, savoring the experiences she had on the way. A minister's daughter, she hoped to attend college the following year and to major in psychology. Her relaxed nature seemed a perfect fit for our needs.

Having secured a thirteen-inch TV between the front seats, I made a comfortable bed of blankets and pillows for the children on the floor of our rented minivan the night before we started our trek. They both clambered over the cushioned floor to claim their spots. Alyona sat propped against the back seat. Alec lay on his stomach on top of two thick sofa pillows. Giggling, they pretended to turn the TV on. I was buoyed by what I interpreted as their eager anticipation of our upcoming trip.

We set out at dawn. Typical for July in the Mid-Atlantic, the humidity already hung heavy in the air. I half-carried, half-steered the sleepy children outside and laid them on the van's cushioned floor, tucked them under their favorite quilt and said a silent prayer: "Please let them sleep a long time. Please let this trip not be a mistake."

Traffic was light as we headed west on I-64. Even the tunnels under the harbor were clear, which I saw as a good omen. The children slept as we crossed the coastal plain, passed Richmond, and climbed the Piedmont toward the Blue Ridge. They stirred only as we neared Charlottesville, home to "Mr. Jefferson's University." Voices in the back announced they were hungry.

We took the next exit for McDonald's, loaded up on bacon and egg biscuits, and got back on the road. Disney songs emanated from the back seat. We climbed the Blue Ridge, descended its west face to the Shenandoah Valley. I drank in the scenery. Talia read her book.

Time passed. Then, somewhere between Roanoke and Blacksburg, Alyona and Alec could take their confinement no longer. They were watching a video of "The Little Mermaid," and at about the point at which Sebastian, Flounder and Scuttle were trying to get Ariel and Eric to kiss so that Ariel would become human, shoes, pillows, videos and books become projectiles behind me. A book hit me in the back of the skull.

Although most of the children's argument was in Russian, it was interspersed with enough English to recognize a classic American back-seat skirmish. "I hate you," one said. "You're mean," said the other. "Stop!" cried both. Talia climbed into the back to separate the combatants amid shouts of "Stop biting," and "Stop pulling hair!" Suddenly, the focus of the violence shifted to Talia.

I pulled off at the next exit and into an empty parking lot. Before I'd brought the van to a full stop, Alyona opened the sliding door and leaped out. She sprinted around the parking lot, cackling, daring me to chase her. I fell for it and rushed her. She darted away.

Breathing deep, fighting to contain my anger, I stalked back to the van. Alyona swooped at me from behind and shoved me in the back. I ignored her. She darted close to kick me in the leg. I ignored her, repeating to myself: "Don't play her game. Don't play her game."

Talia was sitting on the van's floor, arms around Alec. He was sweating and red-faced but no longer screaming. I gave each a cold bottle of water from the cooler and a paper towel to wipe away the sweat.

"Ha, Ha! I win! I win!" Alyona taunted me from the far side of the van. She kicked the tires. I ignored her.

I climbed into the van beside Talia and Alec and opened a cold water. The sun beat down on the vehicle and heat radiated up from the concrete below. No shade, no breeze, relieved the heat. I poured water on Alec's neck then I stepped outside intending to close the sliding door and fire up the engine, so that we could run the air conditioner. Alyona, like a predator stalking its prey, crouched at the bumper observing my every move. For a moment, a fraction of a moment, Alec drew my attention—he raised his water bottle and said, "More." Alyona pounced.

She punched me with uncontrolled rage. She was angry about the long trip. She was angry at yet another "move." She was angry at not understanding what was going on. And she was unbearably afraid. I grabbed at her wrists. She bit hard on my hand. Using a move similar to one I had learned to rescue a drowning swimmer, I grabbed her right wrist with one hand, with the other her waist, and gave her a spin so that she faced away from me, an arm crossed over her chest. Sitting down on the van's floor, I locked my legs around hers and held on.

She threw her head back, landing a solid blow on my nose; then did it again. I bobbed as best as I could and pulled her arms tighter, but the blows kept coming. Tears welled in my eyes. She was strong and determined and persisted for ten minutes before she turned suddenly into a rag doll. The screaming and head butts stopped. With the help of the therapist I had come to understand that Alyona was confident that I would abandon her like her birth mother and her first adoptive mother, and constantly tested me. It gave her a hand in what she reckoned to be inevitable. The most important consequence right now was not punishment for misbehavior, which she fully expected and to which she had become emotionally immune, but reassurance and unconditional love no matter what. She had to believe that she was so important to me that I would not abandon her. Giving her unconditional love was also a surprise move, one that she wasn't quite sure how to deal with. Ultimately, I figured, consistency would win out, and having learned trust, she'd have a healthier appreciation for punishment. Infants start learning trust around nine months of age; Alyona was substantially behind the norm acquiring this vital building block for emotional stability.

She welcomed the bottle of water I offered her and lay down on the blankets. Oh, how I wished I knew what she thought and felt. As Belle in Disney's Beauty and The Beast said, "There's something in him that I simply didn't see."

We arrived at our destination in the foothills of the Smokies in the early evening. Our wood-frame time-share was a split level with two bedrooms (one with a double bed and one with twin beds) and two full baths. A large, well-used fireplace was the focal point of the living room. Being an early riser, I took the sofa bed in the living room, and gave Talia the double bed downstairs.

Alyona and Alec bounced between the twin beds, giggling, while I unpacked their luggage. Alyona's violence during the trip seemed like a fast-fading bad dream; it was in such contrast to the playful, joyous young girl before me. How could the same body hold such wide-ranging moods, such contradictions?

They both cuddled against me as I read from <u>Green Eggs and Ham</u>. Although they understood very little of the actual story, they were enthralled by my shifts in tone as I read, "I do not like green eggs and ham, Sam I am." They clapped and repeated, "Sam I am." It was rare that anyone read them a story in the orphanage. To cuddle at the same time—unimaginable!

Soon they were dozing. I tucked them in under crisp, clean sheets and lay beside Alyona until their steady breathing signaled that they were sound asleep.

After a hearty breakfast of toast, kielbasa and what the children called "yellow eggs" (scrambled), we headed to Fall Creek Falls State Resort Park, a 20,000-acre preserve that takes its name from a 256-foot cascade, one of the highest east of the Rocky Mountains. We all wore good walking shoes and carried backpacks loaded with peanut butter sandwiches, cookies, pretzels, sliced apples, grapes, crackers and bottled water. The warmth of the day was tempered by a periodic breeze and the shade trees that lined the way to our destination, the swinging bridge at 95-foot Piney Falls. I expected the children to glory in nature as I did. I so wanted that.

Alec was the first to find a fallen branch that he judged a fine walking stick. It was far too tall for him, but he insisted that I not shorten it. He strode to the front of our small pack. Alyona found her own stick a few minutes later, and flaunted it before Alec as if to say, "Mine is better than yours."

Peace prevailed, however. We hiked on, pausing now and then to admire butterflies, blooming wildflowers and intricately twisted and bent trees. Alec followed an especially intriguing butterfly until it landed, and scooped it gently into his cupped hands. He held it for Alyona to see, then opened his hands to release it. Alyona did not yet understand gentle. She would stalk a butterfly and, when it landed, slam her hands shut around it. Luckily, the butterflies were quicker than she was.

Before long we arrived at Piney Creek Bridge, near an overlook of the falls. The view was awe-inspiring, the cascade's voice like thunder. I felt privileged to have an audience with such a powerful gift of nature. The children had recently learned a new word and used it now, "WOW," they said. "WOW."

I led them towards the swinging Piney Creek Bridge. Seventy years old, it stretched 350 feet across a densely wooded gorge. The walkway consisted of wooden planks bound by strong cables. The hand rails were cables, too, as were the entire sides. The drooping span cut through a thicket of overarching trees, which blocked any view of its far end. The bridge was both at one with its scenic surroundings and a testament to the resourcefulness and creativity of man.

With a twinge of trepidation, I strode onto the span. It started to sway, and my heart skipped. Then I made the mistake of looking down. What had seemed only moments before one of God's grandest works now threatened: The gorge below was so far down, and this bridge such a wisp of engineering. There was a stiff cross-breeze, what with its open, but cable protected, sides. I gripped both hand-cables. Hoping that the tremor in my voice would not betray me, I invited Talia to join me. "No, thanks," she replied. Had she noticed my white-knuckle hold on the cables?

"I brave," Alec announced as he marched to the bridge.

He gingerly placed one foot on the plank floor while grasping both hand cables, then stepped on with his other foot. The bridge was motionless. Excited, he released both handholds and clapped. Now the bridge gave a sudden swing leftward. Alec's eyes widened. He issued a shriek and clamped onto the cables. "Don't step fast," I coaxed him. "One foot at a time. You can do it." I inched backwards so that I could face him. Focusing on Alec kept my gaze from the ravine.

He walked towards me. Each time he shifted a foot, the bridge swayed and the cables creaked. I could see Alyona back on terra firma, her hands half-covering her eyes. Alec and I timed our movements to the rhythm of the bridge's swings, becoming part of it.

Fifteen feet out, I let go of the cables and clapped vigorously. "You did it," I hollered. Alec's grin stretched across his entire face.

I was no longer intimidated by the bridge's swinging. Like a sailor with sea legs, I was able to maintain my balance without fear or even thought—at least until Alec decided to dash back towards Alyona, which sent the suspended structure into a frenzy of jerks and shudders. I held fast to the cables, electing to stay put until the bridge calmed and I could ease myself back.

I returned to the group to find Alec speaking urgently in Russian to Alyona. The only piece I understood was Alyona's insistent "Nyet, nyet." She yanked her hand away when he tried to take it. I realized that he was trying to persuade her to walk onto the bridge, and reassuring her that it was safe, that he would go with her. I felt it best to leave this to the two of them.

Alec was persistent. Several times he left Alyona and walked several feet onto the bridge, taking care to move slowly, so as to avoid any swaying. Each time, Alyona would step a little closer but stop short of the planking. Undeterred, Alec would pat her on the back, pat the ground and then pat the bridge's floor boards. I had no idea what he was saying, but it must have made sense to Alyona, because she finally took his hand and walked with him to the crossing. He carefully planted her left hand on the cable hand-hold. Then, holding her right hand, his own on the right cable, he took a step forward. Alyona stood fast. Alec bent his head directly in front of her, looked into her eyes and quietly spoke more Russian. Alyona put one foot onto the board; Alec stepped forward with both feet. The bridge rocked slightly. More words from Alec, and now Alyona placed both feet solidly on the wood planks. The bridge rocked more; Alyona stiffened. Alec was still until the swaying stopped. I could see that Alyona's grip had tightened, but Alec paid it no mind. He stood straighter and taller and stared directly ahead; he must have been demonstrating how to keep her eyes to the front, not down. He had gained her trust, and she followed his instructions. Together they embarked across the bridge in baby steps. Soon, Alyona was grinning. They ventured twenty feet out over the abyss, holding hands. When they reversed course for their return, I could see the excitement in their eyes and hear it in their tone. They walked confidently, easy with the bridge's gentle rocking. Alec had achieved a trust way beyond anything I could have pulled off. As soon as they stepped off the bridge they shouted, jumped up and down and raised their hands high. They exchanged high fives.

We spread a blanket on a nearby rock overlooking the grand view and feasted on peanut butter sandwiches. Talia and I layered the children in accolades.

I had learned from painful experience that Alec and Alyona functioned best on a loose schedule, so that they could spontaneously decide how to pass their time. Being somewhat of a compulsive planner who enjoys being busy, I had to make a conscience effort to relax and do nothing.

"But there's so much to see and do," my internal driving voice would shout.

"The children don't care," my reality check would counter.

"I don't want them to miss out on seeing all these new things." The driven side.

"The children don't care. They just want to relax and have fun. They don't want a schedule," insisted my conscience.

I can be stubborn. It required several failures, defined by severe outbursts involving one or both of the children, for me to understand and accept that "less is more." I still researched our destinations and gathered information on all activities or sites available in the vicinity; this satisfied my compulsiveness. Then, like an English professor reading a term paper, I studied all the potential opportunities and red-inked those to be eliminated. It was a methodical and effective way to scale back my own expectations for our excursions. I had practiced this routine for the Tennessee trip in hopes of thwarting any severe blow-ups. Perhaps many were, indeed, averted. But not all.

We had had a leisurely day of sleeping late, swimming, ice cream cones, movies and TV—a recovery day after our long hike. As we prepared for bed, Alyona became giddy and infantile in her behavior. She bounced from bed to bed, taunting both Alec and me. "You bad. You bad. I hate you," she chanted in a high-pitched sing-song, pointing at both of us.

I tried to ignore her. "Let's just brush your teeth," I told Alec.

As we walked out the bedroom door, a pillow smashed me solidly in the head. Alyona clapped. I tossed the pillow back at her.

A hair brush whizzed past my head and banged into the wall. Alyona was now off the bed and frantically clawing all the clothes out of the dresser.

"Stop, Alyona," I pleaded, then asked Talia to take care of Alec. I turned back towards Alyona just in time to duck a glass she had flung. I lunged towards her but was unable to avoid the chair she had kicked into my path.

"Ouch" was all I could muster as I clumsily lost my balance trying to step over wooden legs, seat and back. I landed facedown on the bed. Alyona let out a savage scream and I rolled over just as she landed hard on me. I grabbed her arms. She spit at me. Thick, warm spittle sprayed onto my cheek. I pulled her closer, hoping I could cross her arms in a pin. She bit me and despite myself I reflexively released her wrists. Now she rained roundhouse punches on my face, chest, and neck, all the while screeching in Russian.

I ducked my head, slammed it into her mid-section, and bolted upright, pushing her backwards in the process. She was startled, unsure of my next move, and her hesitation gave me an opening to grab her by her waist and tuck her on my left hip so I could carry her like a football. I ignored her shrill "No, no!" I ignored the painful bruise on my shin from hitting the chair, and the still-smarting bite on my right arm, and the thumping I'd taken to my face. I focused only on getting to the bathroom.

Once there, I knelt to the floor by the tub, still holding Alyona on my hip. I turned on the cold water. In one swift and smooth motion, I grabbed her waist with both hands and swung her under the shower head. The stream was icy cold. She covered her face with her hands and stomped her feet. Her screaming turned to crying, muffled by the shower's spray.

"Calm down, Alyona, calm down," I sputtered, as I leaned into the tub to steady her, and water gushed over my head, into my eyes and mouth.

I caught a glimpse of Talia and Alec standing at the bathroom door. Alec, wide-eyed, was hugging her closely. Perhaps he feared he was next. Perhaps he feared such bizarre behavior in this strange person he was to call mommy. Perhaps it reminded him of the orphanage. Right then I couldn't worry about his 'perhapses'.

After five minutes, Alyona relaxed. She stood soaked through and shivering, anger gone. She understood no better than I what had just happened. "No more, mommy," she whimpered. Dripping wet myself, I lifted her out of the tub and held her close. I felt a swirl of emotions—receding anger, compassion, total confusion. I might never fully decipher the enigma of this complex, damaged girl, but I'd always do my best to offer her comfort. "I love you, Alyona," I told her.

Talia put a "Little Mermaid" nightgown on the only dry spot in the bathroom, the sink. Alyona was complacent and helpful as I dried her off. She insisted that we wipe the floor dry before she got into her gown. It was as if by doing so, she could totally separate from the hellion of a few minutes before, an experience that already seemed more imagination than fact.

We all cuddled in bed as I read the story of Snow White and the Seven Dwarfs. Alec liked Sneezy and Dopey and Alyona, naturally, was enamored with the princess. I caught Alyona stealing a glimpse of herself in the mirror before snuggling beneath the covers.

∽

Near our vacation's end, we drove to Chattanooga to see an old friend of mine, Betty, a creative spirit who'd spent years working with troubled children. I had shown the kids pictures of the Tennessee Aquarium and the animals it contained, and we headed into the city's center with great anticipation. Betty was waiting for us. As we passed into the aquarium's inner sanctum, its mammoth glass walls all that divided us and the water creatures, we were swept into complete communion with fish, mammals, reptiles and amphibians. When Alyona and Alec poked their heads into the glass bubbles protruding into the mammoth tank, they not only were eye-to eye with the barracudas, stingrays and sharks but were one with them. They were Ariel and Sebastian from "The Little Mermaid."

We gawked at the paddlefish, an ancient creature that has been swimming the Mississippi River and its tributaries for thousands of years. Its paddle, covered with taste buds and nerve endings, also acts as a stabilizer while the fish feeds open-mouthed along the surface. I was shocked at learning that the piranha is primarily vegetarian, except during dry seasons, when scarce plant food forces it to seek meat. Alec especially liked the fire-bellied toad with its camouflage of green and black markings. When threatened, the toad shows its brightly colored belly as a warning to would-be predators of its toxic skin secretions. We all delighted in watching the river otters belly-slide down wet slopes and splash about with what seemed an almost eagerness to please. They sometimes peered directly at us through the glass as if to say, "Did you like that? I can do more."

We all left invigorated. Driving to a restaurant, Betty and I talked with the easy intimacy of friends who saw each other every day, rather than once every several years, as was our case. Unfortunately, as we caught up, we became oblivious to the children's activities in the back seat.

Suddenly, I heard the van's sliding door open. I glanced back to see Alec lying on the floor waving his arms through the open door at the car beside us. Alyona was laughing and clapping. We were in the midst of heavy downtown traffic, boxed in the middle lane. Betty was out of her seat in a flash and headed into the back. "I've got him," she said as she latched onto his waistband.

I flicked on my right turn signal and hit the horn, and a driver in the next lane made room for me. "Hold on, I'm turning quickly," I warned Betty, who then braced her feet against the side of the vehicle. I swerved in front of the accommodating driver and stopped at the curb. Betty slid the door shut.

For all the excitement, we arrived at the restaurant unscathed and were told that our wait would be about fifteen minutes. Betty and I settled into the lobby's comfortable arm chairs, taking deep breaths. A mélange of aromas hung in the air—fried onions, barbeque, garlic, fresh bread. I could hear the sizzling of steak or fajita. I was hungrier by the minute.

Then, just as I'd regained my sense of calm, the restaurant was rent by an insistent and extremely loud alarm. The maitre d' hurried in our direction. "What's happened?" he hollered. "What's on fire?"

He made a bee-line for a pull-down fire alarm handle near the entrance. Standing next to it was Alyona, holding her ears and every few seconds clapping her hands. Alec rushed over to join her.

I was right behind the maitre d'. "I'm sorry, sir. I'm sorry," I told him. "They were just adopted from Ukraine and don't understand a lot of English." I stepped between Alyona and the man.

"Announce that it's a false alarm. There is no fire," he told his staff, as he shut off the alarm. He turned to me. "We'll seat you now," he glared.

I walked with lowered head to our table. A few of our fellow diners pointed. Others exchanged quiet comments as they eyed our every move. Alyona and Alec, though, walked tall behind me, quite proud at having created such a scene. Eating cheeseburgers was somewhat anticlimactic after so grand an entrance. But at this point in our Tennessee vacation, I was of the opinion that anticlimax has its merits. As Timon and Pumba in "The Lion King" would say, "Hakuna Matata."

Chapter 11

The paradox of that summer was that as Alyona's language and socialization improved, so did her ability to create havoc. She was becoming fluent in English, which she spoke without an accent. She was almost preternaturally observant and insightful. She was bright, and quick, and had an excellent memory. But she was also tireless in her demands, and with increasing frequency started trouble purely for the pleasure of the challenge.

Alec, on the other hand, was much more receptive to gentleness. He repeated kindergarten and now seemed eager to participate in classroom activities. Music both stirred and calmed him. Due to his limited English, though, he was often baffled and confused by instructions or rules.

He tried too hard to be liked and accepted, which sometimes resulted in other children viewing him as strange. Having been a friend to all at the orphanage, this rejection hurt deeply. It especially affected his behavior in the after-school program: If playfulness did not achieve acceptance, he decided, he'd revert to aggression encouraged by Alyona. That only made matters worse.

I made a decision that turned out to be a defining moment for Alec—I switched him into a tiny, in-home after-school program, separate from Alyona. There were only two other children, an infant and a boy near Alec's age. He and Alec loved jumping on the trampoline, were awed by tanks of Beta fish in the bathroom. His confidence soared in this homey environment. He was accepted and liked. He grew resistant to Alyona's influence.

Alyona advanced to first grade, but her behavior became more unmanageable. She seemed intent on distracting the class. She would climb under and over desks and crawl on the floor, scattering supplies. Her teacher, Ms. Jones, cared for all of her students; none went home without a hug. She was skilled at keeping her class's attention while trying to return Alyona to the group. It was like watching border collies guiding stray sheep back to the flock while keeping the large group in place. Ms. Jones addressed Alyona's disruptions with compassion.

Things got worse, however. Alyona's giddiness and eruptions multiplied at home. She became more self-destructive. She chewed thick chunks of skin from her fingers and toes, and scratched her arms until they bled. She broke a glass vase and superficially sliced her wrists with the shards. She slammed her head against the wall.

The evening sitter, a neighbor girl whom the kids loved, had her hands ever more full. Alyona became obstinate with Rebecca. She relished throwing down the gauntlet almost more than she did play. She seemed to thrive on chaos, on disharmony, on bedlam. Most often, the event sparking one of her blow-ups was quickly forgotten, and replaced by agitation for its own sake. Rebecca's father often had to come to the house to restore order.

It was the fish, though, that really jolted me. Alec's sitter called one evening to report that she'd found her blue Beta fish torn in half, floating in its fish bowl, and her orange fish missing. She knew Alec liked the fish and didn't think he would hurt them, but she had no other explanation. I suddenly recalled Alyona going to the bathroom when we had picked up Alec and I knew what had happened.

After speaking with the therapist and arranging to see her the next day, I had the sitter put the torn fish in a jar so I could take it with us. Alyona and Alec were not informed of the call from the sitter or why we were making the special trip to Patsy's. They did not know what I was carrying in the bag, either.

At the therapist, the bag was placed on the table. At the appropriate time, Patsy opened the bag revealing the torn fish in the jar. Alec gasped. Alyona was unfazed. As if she had simply torn a page of paper, Alyona calmly described how she had torn one fish in two and flushed the other down the toilet. Her remorse amounted to a blasé shrug of her shoulders. She offered no hint of shame. It was incomprehensible to her that we should be so upset. Her crime had absolutely no meaning for her. It was a spontaneous action, and had occurred simply because the fish had had the misfortune of being in her presence.

"Nancy, you and I need to talk," Patsy's face was grim as she scheduled a time for me to return alone to further discuss Alyona's condition.

When I met with Patsy a few days later, I felt a heaviness in my chest and a deep sense of doom. Had I failed Alyona? Would Patsy say Alyona needed to be removed from my home, that she could never heal? I was on the verge of tears when Patsy summoned me from the waiting room.

"Alyona is a very sick little girl," Patsy began. "She needs more intensive therapy than you or anyone else can provide in the home." She recognized my fear and worry. "It's not your fault, Nancy," she reassured me. "In fact, I think you're the perfect home for her. A lot of people would have quit by now. I absolutely believe Alyona can get better and live a fulfilling life, but it is going to take a lot of hard work and a long time."

"I'll do whatever you say, Patsy." Tears rolled down my cheeks as I struggled to speak. The office seemed hot and airless—it had never felt this way at previous sessions. I knew we were at a watershed moment; I willed myself to be clinical, objective. I knew that was the only way I could best handle the critical decisions that lay ahead.

I swallowed hard and sat straighter on the sofa. "OK, Patsy, what do I need to do?" I function best when I'm focused and have a plan.

"We need to select a residential facility for Alyona," Patsy said. "She is getting worse, and when she hits the wall we want to be able to move her quickly to the best place for her."

"She'll feel abandoned again. Won't that make it worse?"

"She may, but she can't continue like this," Patsy said. "She needs intensive treatment. I know you, Nancy," she said. "You won't give up on Alyona and you'll do everything humanly possible to be sure she knows that." She handed me a paper with a name, The Bridges, on it. "I've researched some places for you, and I believe this is the best. They're expecting a visit from you and Alyona. I think you'll feel better when you meet the people and see the facility."

I nodded my assent.

Chapter 12

The exhaust from the Greyhound buses irritated my throat and sinuses. My parents and I stood in line while I waited to board a bus for the twenty-four hour trip from Orlando to Virginia, where I would start my freshman year at Lynchburg College. It was a small, liberal arts school affiliated with The Disciples of Christ church, of which I was a member. My older brother, a rising senior and student leader, had left for Lynchburg a week earlier to prepare for freshman orientation. He had always raved about the school's faculty, the small classes, the positive attitudes of students and staff alike, and how wonderful it felt that everyone knew you and treated you like family. I felt excited and cocky and incredibly self-reliant as I prepared to embark alone on the long trip.

The bus driver took my ticket. I hugged my parents, climbed the steps into the bus, turned and waved goodbye. It was August 1964.

Thirty-six years later, I felt nothing but dread as I again made my way to Lynchburg. At Patsy's suggestion, and in anticipation that long-term placement may be needed in the not-too-distant future, I was taking Alyona to The Bridges so we could see the facility and meet the staff. My hope was that this preliminary acquaintance would ease Alyona's fears should placement be necessary. Mary Lou, a friend from church, and I drove Alyona the nearly five hours to The Bridges. Its reputation for professional and effective treatment of children was irreproachable: Both individual and group therapy was extensive and its staff focused on creating a family-like environment. Its approach was consequence-based using a point system, and it had forged relationships with organizations in the surrounding community so the children could participate in a wide range of activities. The Bridges had no fences or walls. Therapy staff was on the job twenty-four hours a day. Patsy highly recommended the program. We should seek acceptance for Alyona ahead of time, she suggested, so if placement became necessary Alyona could be quickly admitted.

I wrestled with my emotions as we neared the place. The words, "We are family and we stick together in good and bad times," came back to haunt me. What message would I be sending to Alyona if I placed her at The Bridges? I wanted to help her tortured spirit heal. I wanted her to embrace life and herself and to fear neither. I wanted her laughter to be heartfelt and unguarded. I wanted her to know the comfort and security of belonging and being loved.

Mary Lou had worked with youth programs for years, and she kept Alyona's attention for the trip's first couple of hours. Alyona was intrigued by a birth mark on Mary Lou's cheek and giggled every time Mary Lou would point to it and, with saucy pride, say, "It's my beauty mark."

But after dinner at Hardee's, Alyona bolted out of the restaurant and raced in the dark into a nearby neighborhood. Mary Lou and I walked the lot, peering into the gloom. Every so often, Alyona would dash past us, screaming, and disappear into a darkened yard or alley. She soon became irked that we weren't aggravated enough to chase after her; and turned to a more dangerous strategy: As a car came down the street, she darted directly into its path and stopped.

I decided to play by her rules. I sprinted as fast as I could towards her. She squealed and promptly ran across the street to safety. I stayed after her, just a step or two behind.

When she concluded she couldn't shake me, she stopped, spun around and lashed at me with fists and feet. I hardly felt the hair-pulling as I hoisted her football-style under an arm and carried her to the car. I was oblivious to neighborhood onlookers.

Mary Lou opened the car. I tossed Alyona into the back seat and locked the door. At first, she satisfied her anger by kicking the back of my seat and pulling my hair, despite Mary Lou's attempts to stop her. Alyona's anger, though, required greater release.

She turned her attention to the car's headliner, tearing at the fabric. As her nails were chewed very short, she used pencils to rip holes so she could then pull strips of lining away. Soon pieces of carpet succumbed to her attack. She tossed the ruined material into the front seat and hooted with pride at her accomplishment. I drove on, wishing the car had wings. When the entire ceiling had been stripped of lining, Alyona settled contentedly in her seat and fell fast asleep.

The Bridges seemed all that its champions had made it out to be. It had the look and feel more of a small college campus than a mental health facility. Children played, rode bikes and skateboards or talked in a grassy, unfenced courtyard.

The counselors and therapists we met were cheery and interactive. The cabins boasted sturdy but attractive cargo furniture. The interiors were colorful and homey. Meals were served family style in a sunny dining hall. The classrooms accommodated about six students each and were led by certified teachers. Nurses were on hand around the clock. They were professional, caring and responsive to my questions. A couple of them had retired from public health. They all had easy smiles. It was readily apparent that the staffers believed in what they were doing. I knew I could feel comfortable with Alyona being placed here if the need arose.

"Come quickly," the voice on the phone said. "Alyona has had a meltdown and we've had to evacuate all the other children from her classroom."

I hurried to her first-grade classroom to find her sitting with her teacher, Ms. Jones, on the floor, both of them calmly eating lunch. But evidence of a just-passed storm was all about them: Papers and books were strewn all over the room. Chairs, shelves and tables were lying on their sides. Hundreds of crayons were scattered on the rug.

I navigated past the obstacles to Alyona's side. She avoided eye contact. Alyona had become very giddy, agitated and hyperactive shortly after arriving at school, Ms. Jones told me. She'd refused to sit at her desk or on the beanbag in the reading corner. She'd insisted on constantly interrupting Ms. Jones and drawing on the chalkboard. She'd crawled on the floor and tried to flip students' desks when they refused to join her. She'd thrown shoes, toys and stuffed animals. She'd talked and sung constantly.

The more Ms. Jones had tried to ignore her, the louder and wilder she had become. Her classmates had cowered, covering their heads. Some had crawled closer to Ms. Jones. Alyona had tried to push them away. Finally, the administrators had pulled all of the other children from the classroom and taken them to an early lunch.

As soon as I began speaking to Alyona, she again erupted. "Ha, ha, ha," she singsonged. "I made a mess." She threw her remaining French fries at me and kicked the toys my way. I took a step closer. She darted under a nearby desk, hurling crayons and wads of paper. "I'm so sorry for the interruption," I told Ms. Jones. A toy truck bounced off my side and a stuffed rabbit hit me in the face. It was time to leave, I told Alyona. "School is finished for the day." I reached out my hand for hers, hoping we could walk to the car. She didn't want to leave. She told me to go back to work. "No," I said, "You and I are going to visit Patsy." I had conferred with the therapist enroute to the school, and Patsy had cleared her schedule so she could see us at once.

When I tried escorting her to the car, she bolted down the hall. It took both Ms. Jones and I to corner her. We carried her kicking and screaming through the halls, tossed her into the car's back seat, and I tried to get behind the wheel before she opened a window or door. She was too fast: She managed to partially drop a window before I could lock it.

I started the car and gunned it for the expressway. Alyona kicked the seats and pulled my hair from the back seat, threw whatever she could find at me or the windshield. I kept an eye on the rear-view mirror while we sped down the interstate, ducking when I could, fending off hits I saw coming.

Alyona snaked an arm through the cracked window, twisted it down to the door's exterior handle, and fumbled with the button. I grabbed her other arm and jerked her away, causing her to fall on one knee between the seats. I briefly thought about pulling onto the shoulder and calling 911 for help, but then I envisioned her making a mad dash into the speeding traffic.

Instead, I maintained my grip on her arm, knowing that it truly could mean the difference between life and death. She bit my hand, kicked the seat and pulled my hair, but I didn't let go.

We made record time getting to Patsy's office. Alyona was sullen and suspiciously calm as she got out of the car. She glared at me but said nothing. We took the elevator to Patsy's floor. When we stepped off, she suddenly threw herself onto her stomach, beat the floor with her fists, and shouted, "I hate you. I hate you." I tried to pick her up. She spit at me and swung at my face. A man and woman leaving a neighboring office stared in disbelief, then hurried around us into the elevator. I knelt beside Alyona and stroked her head. "It'll be all right," I tried to reassure her. She kept screaming, "I don't want to see Patsy." A young woman who had been sitting in the waiting area approached, asking, "What can I do to help?"

"Get Patsy," I cried.

I heard Patsy half-running down the hall. She crouched on the floor next to Alyona. "You can do it," she said, gently but firmly. "You can stand up on your own and we'll walk back to my office together." Alyona stopped screaming and stood up. She pushed my hand away when I offered it. Calmly, with head bowed, she led the way.

In Patsy's office Alyona was giddy, moved constantly, seemed driven to touch every surface around her, every object. She could not engage in conversation. Her words were gibberish, unrelated to any of our questions. She was not oblivious to our presence, but didn't acknowledge us, either. Occasional flashes of clarity left as quickly as they arrived.

A couple of times, quite unexpectedly, she curled up on my lap and wrapped my arms around her. But she'd stay put for only a minute or so. Patsy confirmed what I feared, "We need to admit her to the psychiatric center," she said," and then make arrangements for admission to The Bridges."

Alyona seemed unmoved when I left her. She was still hyperactive and near as I could tell, blind to what was happening around her. I wasn't much better off: I was in too much emotional shock to feel sadness, regret or fear. The rush of adrenaline I'd experienced in the car on the way to Patsy's had trickled away, leaving me utterly spent. Unlike Alyona, I moved very slowly.

I focused on keeping track of instructions from the staff—"Complete this paperwork," and "Bring her clothes by later tonight."

A psychiatrist walked me through what the center knew so far. "It was the voices," she said. "They were telling Alyona to kill both you and her teacher."

What? How could I possibly digest the thought that this seven-year-old girl was driven by internal voices to kill?

"We are adjusting medications to help stabilize her. But your daughter is a very sick little girl who will need extensive, long-term treatment," the psychiatrist said. "I agree that she should be admitted to The Bridges." Although my heart quailed, I knew that she was right. "I know," I said.

Lugging a small artificial Christmas tree and a bag of wrapped presents, Alec and I made our way to Alyona's room at the end of the hall. It wasn't the most festive of settings—walls a neutral tan, scratched and discolored from previous occupants; ceiling light dim; windows nonexistent; an absence of music, much less Christmas carols.

This was a way station for the bearers of vagrant minds. It was a stopover for children whose homeless emotions burst out on their own directionless journeys. Like switchmen controlling trains, the doctors manipulated medications to enable the children to move forward safely to more permanent types of therapy.

I placed the tree in the middle of Alyona's neatly-made bed, surrounding it with her gifts. "It's going to be beautiful," I said, as I knelt to plug in the lights. Instantly, the lights twinkled. "Hurray," I said. "Merry Christmas." I managed an exaggerated smile. "Ho, ho, ho," I chortled as I gave her one of the presents. "Santa left these under the tree for you."

She sat on the pillow, a slight smile evident, and began opening the gifts; she was focused, slowly undoing each strip of tape until she could remove the paper. She neatly laid the gifts in a semicircle around her—a soft, cuddly baby doll with a bottle and diapers, furry pink slippers, and a boom box. "Thanks, mommy," she said. There was no sparkle or fire in her eyes; her expression was a blank.

It was lunch time. Alyona took my hand and led us to a line forming in the hallway. "Come mommy." While we waited, she calmly talked with Alec about Christmas presents. Voices? Kill? Violence? Restlessness? Where were the crevices that cloistered these frightening and unpredictable impulses? How long would it take to find and treat them? A therapist's booming voice brought me back to reality, "Let's go."

We filed into the cafeteria. The only touches of festivity were a cafeteria worker in a Santa hat and quiet Christmas music issuing from the P.A. We ate our ham and vegetables with only intermittent conversation. "How are you feeling, Alyona?" I asked her.

"OK," she said.

"I miss you a bunch."

"Me, too," she replied.

"What do you do during the day?" I asked.

"Watch TV."

"How do you think I'd look with that hat on my nose?" I pointed to the red stocking on the worker's head. She laughed out loud. Alyona was still inside this unfamiliar child. She was simply hidden. There was hope.

I felt tremendous sadness for a seven-year-old girl whose innocence had been so unfairly hijacked. I wanted to rip out those devil-like voices that frightened and controlled her. I wanted to wrap Alyona in the fleece-like comfort of softness and love. I wanted to cauterize those ugly memories that made her strike out. I wanted to say, "Come back home and live happily ever after." If only I could.

Alyona came home the next day. That night I laid beside her and held her hand. We stared at the ceiling, neither of us speaking. I worried about the next day's trip to The Bridges. I searched for the right words to reassure her that I was not abandoning her. When she broke the silence, she caught me off guard: "Mommy, when I die, will I go to heaven?" My God, I thought, did she think she was going to die? I squeezed her hand. "Hon, you are already one of God's favorite angels," I said, groping. "That's why he asked me to take extra good care of you. So you'll be staying at The Bridges for a while so you can get well and feel better." It was the best I could do. It probably helped me more than it did her.

The next day, Alyona, Alec and I headed to Lynchburg. We didn't talk. Alec colored and played with toy cars. Alyona wordlessly played with her doll. Although we had discussed where we were going and what would happen, I don't think either of them truly comprehended that Alyona wouldn't be returning with us. We rolled through bucolic small towns, passed farmland dormant for the winter.

For me, the Blue Ridge Mountains around Lynchburg emit both strength and tranquility. They beckon the adventurer and those seeking spiritual healing. Being in their shadow, their peaks rising dark and steep above me, has always given me a sense of safety and security. I prayed they continued to mean that for me, and would come to represent a haven for my daughter, too.

It didn't take long enough to unload Alyona's clothes and personal effects. Alec had carefully drawn a picture, replete with bright yellows, greens and blues, and given it to Alyona to remember him by. I promised Alyona that I'd call and write every day and visit her every week. How empty those promises must have sounded.

Our hugs were all too brief. I took Alec's frail little hand and turned my back to walk away. I found it difficult, physically difficult, to do so. Alyona started to run after us, but was held back by the nurses. "Mommy don't go," she cried. "I'll be good, I promise.

Keep walking, I reminded myself. Don't look back.

"Mommy, please! Please!" Alyona screamed. I looked down at Alec. He was weeping. I squeezed his hand and swallowed hard. Alyona wailed. We reached the door. "I love you, Alyona," I called back to her. "I'll call tonight, Hon."

We stepped outside. The doors closed behind us. I struggled to breathe. My hand shook as I started the car. I held Alec close and we sobbed like two small children who had lost our way in a vast and dark woods.

PART III

Home Away
From Home

Chapter 13

Only the creaking of the garage door defied the monastic quiet as I backed my car down the driveway, pajama-clad Alec asleep in the back seat. The stars hovered bright overhead; dawn was still hours away.

In slightly more than two hours, halfway to Lynchburg, we would stop at Hardee's. We'd park near the eighteen-wheelers in the gravel parking lot, exchange greetings with the usual collection of truck drivers in plaid shirts and baseball caps along with farmers savoring coffee, the restaurant's red-eyed crew. So went our Saturday morning ritual. Alec, yawning and barefoot, would shuffle into the restaurant unsure of where he was. I would tuck clothes, socks and shoes into his folded arms and gently push him into the men's bathroom.

While he changed, I ordered bacon, egg and cheese biscuits for both of us. Alec would reappear with his pajamas balled up in one hand—and wide awake, talkative, hungry.

It only took a couple of months for me to memorize the location of all the public bathrooms, fast-food eateries and gas stations along our route. I knew which ones were open all night, and which opened at six. I knew the one-stoplight towns and the deer crossings. I knew the curves on which police hid to catch the trucks speeding on U.S. 460. I knew where to find the best coffee and the best ice cream cones.

I also learned to appreciate beautiful sunrises over wide-open fields or pastures where horses romped or cattle grazed. I became familiar with the sound of tractors and the smell of newly plowed farmland. I learned that we still raised cotton in Virginia, alongside corn, beans and alfalfa.

I became an aficionado of books-on-tape and could usually "read" an entire book in a weekend. I expanded my traditional mystery genre to include history, biographies and even a few whimsical tales. As the engine hummed, I was transported back in time to my parent's bedroom where my father would entertain me and my siblings for hours by reading us stories of magical adventure, as well as such classics as Heidi, even poetry. As it had then, being read to mesmerized me.

The back seat was Alec's domain. He had pillows, blankets, toys, games, coloring books and crayons back there, and—-not least—a Game Boy and extra batteries. I had valiantly battled to keep the space clean, but over the months surrendered to the apple cores, orange peels and crumbs that materialized between the seat cushions. The car usually had a subtle bouquet of rotting garbage.

Nestled in his seat, Alec would play games and continuously sing. His lyrics tended toward activities of the week, Alyona or meditations on God, bad behavior, and family. He'd sometimes catch my eye as I glanced in the rear-view mirror and say, "I love you Mommy."

One Saturday a mixture of snow and rain welcomed us to Lynchburg. I parked the car in The Bridges' near-empty lot and peered out my window, dreading the cold, when I noticed the rain on the glass. Small droplets merged into larger tributaries that trickled down the glass, feeding a large pool at the base. It was entrancing, then enlightening: Suddenly I saw that Alyona, Alec and I were that pool, constantly nourished by many tributaries of support, love and strength. Nature, the teacher!

Throughout Alyona's stay at The Bridges, I grew expert at using the internet to locate nearby events or activities—if it happened within two hours of Lynchburg, we'd be there. The caveat was that Alyona had to earn points by exhibiting good behavior in order to spend any time outside of the facility.

We ate garlic-flavored jellies, dips, breads and cheese. We rode horses. We discovered a small but fascinating Indian museum in the woods, where the proprietors showed us pictures of their grandparents, great-grandparents and other relatives in traditional regalia during pow-wows.

We ate pancakes and barbecue at church socials, dropped in on neighborhood celebrations, historical events, and good-harvest rituals, and hit every small-town fair in that part of the state.

In the summer Alyona and Alec played archaeologist at Poplar Forest, Thomas Jefferson's retreat, learned how to make bricks, dressed in period clothes.

A place we visited often was downtown Lynchburg's Amazement Children's Museum, where touching the exhibits was encouraged, which certainly relieved me of any anxiety. We all climbed the Amazement Tower, the tallest indoor climbing structure in the country. It extended through all four floors and into the observatory deck on the roof.

"You can't catch us, Mom," Alec and Alyona would taunt, as they embarked on the maze of slides, ladders, tunnels and zip line.

I'd dutifully chase after them, but most often had to concede to their agility and quickness—unless I cheated and took the glass elevator, and ambushed them up top.

My favorite exhibit was the Amazing Body, where we could walk through a heart and learn the functions of the circulatory and respiratory systems. Alyona and Alec weren't quite as enthusiastic about it as I was. Alec's favorite was the Pedal power, where we could race each other on stationary bikes while scenes of the Blue Ridge Mountains were projected onto a screen before us. Alyona was drawn to the Imagination Studio, which was filled with craft supplies. She would sit at a work table cutting colored paper into various shapes that she'd glue into whimsical collages. Her images were always bright. They gave me hope that Alyona's basic nature was cheery and optimistic, in spite of her dreadful outbursts.

On pretty days we hiked or rode bikes along the James River, on trails that followed old railroad tracks. We visited a safari park in the

Shenandoah Valley where bison, zebras, reindeer, elk, giraffes and ostriches roamed free. The animals were not the least bit hesitant about coming right up to us and gobbling food from our hands; Alyona's favorite was the zebra.

In the beginning, many weekends were cut short by Alyona's behavior. She might get upset because we had to leave an event or because I wouldn't buy her something she wanted. At times she'd become enraged without any evident reason. She'd bite, scratch and pull hair, scream, and curse. She'd resist getting in the car, or refuse to get out when we returned to The Bridges. If I sought help from the staff, Alyona might dash into the street. Several times she had to be carried inside by the staff while she screamed that she hated them, or called them "you motherfuckers."

I'd watch with tears streaming down my face. These moments were mysteries to me. One minute, she'd be an excited and happy child, eagerly exploring a festival or coloring a masterpiece, and the next this beast.

If such a scene played out on a Saturday, Alec and I would be able to visit her for only thirty minutes the following day. If it occurred on Sunday, we drove home early feeling sad, cheated, bewildered.

One weekend she earned permission for an overnight with family friends in Fincastle. We had stayed at their place a number of times prior to her admission to The Bridges, and Phebe and Jake had visited Alyona in Lynchburg.

The children immediately jumped into a huge pile of sawdust in Jake's workshop, a byproduct of his profession as a master craftsman of intricate, period-replica furniture. In minutes sawdust clung to their clothing, hair, ears, faces. "I've got more on me than you," bragged Alec, whose eyes and mouth were barely visible under a thick coat of oaken curls.

"No you don't," Alyona replied. She took a handful of sawdust and roughly shoved it down Alec's shirt. With that, their laughter morphed to shouting. Both children turned violent.

Without understanding why, I loaded the kids into the car and headed to the Virginia Military Institute in nearby Lexington, Virginia. We arrived in time for the cadets' evening drills, and watched as hundreds of young men and women with bolt-upright posture moved in unison across the parade grounds. A woman gave the orders with a commanding shout. We were spellbound.

We toured the museum with guidance from cadets in crisp uniforms, their strides measured and sharp, their speech direct and respectful.

"Do you think they would treat their mothers like you two just did to me?" I asked the kids. I knew my approach was not exactly in accord with therapeutic theory, but I was desperate. How do you teach children the nature of respect? Of restraint?

"No, Mom," they replied. "Let's try it again."

On our return to Phebe and Jake's, two contrite children played without fighting, spoke politely and frequently mentioned the "soldiers in uniform" who had looked so tall and important. Alyona and Alec carried sticks and marched around the yard, doing their best to keep in synchronous step. This unconventional intervention made for a very pleasant weekend.

Chapter 14

We constantly listened to music in the car, and we politely tolerated each other's selections—or tried to, anyway. Alec had Vacation Bible School tapes that he insisted on playing ad nauseum. They were full of catchy tunes of the sort that imprint themselves on the brain, and replay in your head despite, or because of, your efforts to forget them. "Hey, pardner, have some beans"—this was a refrain in a Western-themed song that always brought laughter to Alec as he sang it in the car.

Alyona's tastes ran to boy bands and love songs. When the kids were distracted, I might try to slip in some classical, country or easy-listening. Because music was our common pleasure, I decided to make a tape for each of them, consisting of an eclectic mix of songs. I did this for Mother's Day, telling them, "You can play the tape and remember how much I love you."

There was the whimsical kindergarten song "When the Cows Come Home," the Carpenters' "Bless the Beast and the Children" and a favorite, Cassidy's "Wade in the Water." But the song that resonated most was that of country music singer, Sara Evans' "I Could Not Ask for More." When that came on the radio, the children almost reflexively cranked up the volume.

The tune, rhythm and vocals were seductive, but it was the lyrics that captured the children's attention. It's more than a love song, but an affirmation of a complete and fulfilling relationship:

Lying here with you
Listening to the rain
Smile just to see the smile upon your face
These are the moments I thank God that I'm alive
And these are the moments I'll remember all my life
I've found all I've waited for
And I could not ask for more

I liked the song and the feeling it gave me; that's why I included it on the tape. I was a little surprised, though, by the immediate affinity the children had with it. It spoke to them:

And every prayer has been answered
Every dream I've had's come true
Yeah, right here in this moment
Is right where I'm meant to be
Here with you here with me

If the song was playing when we stopped the car, we sat and listened to the end before I turned off the motor. The children were convinced that Sara Evans was singing the song just for us. It became our rallying tune both when we needed a lift and when we were celebrating a day that had gone well. It described a family's bond in ways I couldn't. It evoked a warm togetherness, whether we three heard it together or separated by 250 miles during the week.

And it prompted Alyona's first tentative steps toward a real connection with me. On one of our daily phone calls, Alyona remarked that she had heard our "family song." It was her first mention of family, a first acknowledgement that she was building a sense of trust, a casual reference to the possibility of love. My heart sang.

I've found all I've waited for

And I could not ask for more

There were other signals of progress. The Bridges held a special family weekend, inviting parents and siblings to spend time in the residents' cottages, which I'd only glanced at prior to Alyona's admission. Now I followed her in. The front door opened onto a living room furnished with a sturdy oak sofa, love seat, and two chairs. Floor-to-ceiling book shelves and a big TV filled one wall. In a corner stood a phone booth. I imagined Alyona there when she took my nightly calls. Sometimes she'd answer only to immediately slam down the receiver. Other nights we would chat the full ten minutes, she describing with excitement her successes of the day (how she didn't get angry, didn't curse, played games with her therapist, earned points to attend the ice cream social), and my optimism about her healing would be buoyed. And some nights she seemed lost in despair, her comments coming in stunted, barely audible phrases.

Across the room was a small kitchenette with a sink, refrigerator, range and microwave. I knew Alyona and her housemates made popcorn and experimented at creating sweets. A hallway led to the bedrooms and bathroom for girls 13 and over, and an alcove next to it was devoted to video games. Alyona said this is where one of the cottage counselors had cut her hair for her. Down a second hallway, this one shorter, were the laundry and the time-out room. The latter was an unfurnished space where children would be sequestered after a tantrum and, as Alyona put it, needed to "chill out." A counselor was always in the room at such times. Alyona had spent her share of time chilling out.

To the left of the front door a hallway led to the bedrooms and bathroom for 6-12-year old residents. Alyona's room was at the end of the hall. I recognized her comforter on one of the two oak beds. It was reversible: One side was covered with dark blue teardrops interspersed with light green leaves. The other side was a mélange of blue squares and splotches of yellow, red, orange and green, all on pale blue. It was a merry assortment of colors.

I hoped she nestled herself in the comforter often, especially on those days that seemed particularly bleak.

Alyona picked up a teddy bear propped against her pillows. I had given it to her. "I sleep with this every night," she told me. "It helps me remember you."

She reached into her closet and pulled out two big shoe boxes, one pink and one blue, filled with cards. Her counselors read them to her, she said, then asked: "Why do so many people write to me? And who is this 'old lady'?" She pointed to a card signed, "An old lady friend of your mom's."

"That's Boots," I told her. "That's her nickname. She lives in Texas. People send these cards because they want you to know that lots of people care about you and want you to get better."

In fact, a day had not gone by—not one—on which she had not received mail. I sent her a card every day and friends, colleagues, relatives and members of my congregation mailed her letters, crafts, knitting and games. The Bridges had never had a patient receive so much mail. It came in such volume that the facility gave Alyona her own mailbox.

She was puzzled by such outpouring of love and concern. She had trouble understanding why strangers would take the time to send her things, regardless of whether she'd been good or bad.

I was overwhelmed by the display. By nature, I shy from seeking help or even admitting that I might need it. I take pride in my self-reliance and independence. A strong introvert, I guard my emotions and fears. But as I watched my daughter spread the cards over her bed and run her fingers over them, I gave a silent thanks for all the people who'd seen through me. And I realized that Alyona was not alone in healing through her experience at The Bridges: I was becoming less afraid of my humanity; I was starting to accept the help of others without seeing it as a weakness.

"This is one of your cards," she said, handing it to me. It had a picture of a cat on the front and it said, "I miss you." Inside were several Meows translated to mean "I love you. Hurry home." The signature, including a pad print, was from Teager, her own cat.

She pointed to another inscription, in my handwriting: "Lots and Lots of love, PG."

"I'm your precious girl," she said. A smile took over her face; she had to close her eyes to make room for it. "Absolutely," I said. I pulled her into a hug.

One of her counselors had told me that on difficult days, when Alyona took to throwing things around her room, she was always careful not to damage her cards. The counselors figured that Alyona felt she didn't deserve love and kindness, and was determined to prove it through her rages - but protecting the cards gave away the progress she was making. Somewhere deep, she was beginning to acknowledge that she might be lovable, might be deserving.

It wasn't always easy to spot this progress. When her teacher, Ms. Jones, and friends from the Roanoke area visited her, she met their unconditional love with ambivalence on good days, and hostility on others. She could not trust their sincerity. Rather than face another rejection, she strove to reject. Her world vacillated from a distorted Picasso to a mellow Monet.

During the winter, Alyona played on The Bridges basketball team, which competed in the Lynchburg city league. The games were held in an old YMCA in a depressed and crumbling corner of the city's downtown.

Alec and I would leave home early enough on Friday afternoons to arrive in time for the evening games. The gym lacked bleachers: chairs were shoved against the wall on three sides of the court. It was a tight fit. My feet usually rested on the outside line, and I'd have to shift sideways to make room for players running down the side. Spectators had to make room for players throwing the ball in. The pungent odor of sweat, from both players and spectators, was notable.

The opposing players made eager attempts at teamwork, passing the ball among themselves, cheering for each other and rarely displaying anger or disappointment over a missed shot.

Let's just say that players on The Bridges team had a contrasting style. They were loathe to pass and quick to hurl criticism. For them, basketball seemed an individual sport: When you got the ball, you kept it; success was measured not so much by the score, but rather by how many times and for how long you held the ball and how many times you threw it at the basket. The kids rarely knew the score, but they knew who'd made a basket. And when they missed a shot, they descended deep into a pit of self-hatred. Recovery was slow. They were accustomed to being wrong, worthless, blamed.

Most of the players had aggressive histories, but were timid on the court. They ambled sloth-like from one end of the court to the other. When directed, they dutifully raised hands over their heads, but that didn't mean they grasped the defensive tactic's value. On occasion, an opposing player was long gone while a Bridges defender remained flat-footed, arms still raised, waving.

Alyona was the youngest and smallest player on the team. She had no previous basketball experience. That did not deter her, though. This was not sport, as she saw it, but an opportunity for attention. And she did her best to get it: She waved her arms in front of opponents, undaunted by the limited effect of her efforts. She knew nothing about dribbling, and was called often for traveling. Occasionally, a loose ball would bounce right to Alyona, who'd cling to it or throw it away in a panic.

Once, while standing near the basket, a rebound fell straight into her arms. She froze startled. As we watched from the sidelines in astonishment, coaches and both teams shouted at her to shoot. "Throw at the basket," a teammate urged. "You can make the shot," an opponent said.

No one tried to steal the ball or to block her; everyone just stood in place, clapping. Coaches and spectators joined in the cheering.

"Go, little girl", I heard someone to the left of me say. I stood and hollered.

She held the ball with both hands, bent at the knees, brought the ball down towards the floor and then with all of her might hurled it underhanded in the direction of the basket. It rose underneath the net, barely touching the rim's underside and fell back to the floor. But the room erupted in applause, just the same. Players from both teams patted her on the back, some even leaving the bench to congratulate her. Alyona walked off the court victorious.

As we pulled into The Bridges parking lot one Saturday morning, Alec was belting out his own rendition of "Wade in the Water." It had been a good ride to Lynchburg; I was enthralled with a P.D. James book-on-tape and wondering how the hero, Adam Dalgliesh, would ever solve a complex murder. We were both in high spirits.

We strolled around the side of the main building. The grounds seemed relaxed: children and staff lolled in the grass. I was envisioning a leisurely hike in a park along the James River, a swim at the Y, maybe a movie. When I appeared at the nurse's station I could tell something was wrong. The two nurses exchanged glances, as if trying to decide who'd go first.

"Alyona had a very rough evening," one of them finally said. "She won't be able to go out this weekend." Alyona had become enraged when she was told to turn off the TV and go to bed, they told me. She kicked the furniture and the staff. Her language was threatening. She bit and pulled hair, and demonstrated strength out of scale for such a small child. Medication had finally quelled the rampage. "I'm sorry we didn't call you regarding the incident," the nurse added, her tone apologetic, "but it was quite late last night." Alyona had not yet wakened, she said, but we could visit with her in the dining room for twenty minutes that afternoon.

I'd heard similar words on several previous visits, but this time they had an unexpected effect on me. I stood silent for several seconds, unable to muster any words beyond "Oh." Without warning, I was wrapped in a shroud of depression, trapped in an airless, windowless corner of my mind where life was doubt. I tried to explain it away to myself: It was fatigue— weekly 500-mile trips had exacted a physical toll that had snuck up on me; I was experiencing the burst-balloon syndrome over the sudden loss of a laughter-filled family weekend that I'd had my heart set on. But reality stabbed through these flimsy rationalizations. Truth was, I was overcome with doubt about Alyona's ability to heal. Beyond doubt, perhaps almost a sudden pessimism. And I felt helpless to change it.

I was angry that Alyona would sabotage our time together, when she knew that Alec and I were putting forth so much effort. And I was angry at myself for being angry, because it was Alyona who had been abused and who was doing the real work of healing. "We'll come back in the afternoon to visit with her," I heard myself saying.

Taking hold of Alec's hand, I forced myself to walk back to the car. As I sat steeped in gloom, Alec studied me from the passenger seat. "Mom, we can still have a good time," he finally said. "And we can bring her a flower from our walk. It'll be OK." Translated: Don't give up!

We decided to hike at a park high above the James. Sidewalks weaved through acres of forest, picnic areas and playgrounds. Standing at the edge of the park, we could see an old railroad trestle stretching from bluff top to bluff top over the river, and imagined the rumble of fast-moving passenger trains carrying families of old to summer vacations or holiday gatherings.

Meanwhile, to our mission, Alec spied what he deemed the perfect flower. He edged down the bluff and, oh so gently, picked it without losing a petal.

Back at The Bridges, we presented it to Alyona. "The flower helps you remember that you are in our hearts all the time," I told her. "This is how we can share the view with you."

I wanted to leave her a more tangible aide memoire, something that could ease her fears. That night I called Pat, and she offered the perfect suggestion. Before visiting Alyona on Sunday, Alec and I made a trip to Wal-Mart. Armed with a bag filled with brightly colored paints, brushes and three pillowcases, we met Alyona in the conference room.

The nurses supplied paper to cover the table. Alyona was intrigued. We each took a pillowcase and set the paints and cups of water in the center of the table. "We'll all paint something special on each other's pillowcases," I explained. "It will help us remember that we are a family with lots of love and we stick together in good and bad times." Everyone immediately started painting, lips pursed. First, we each painted identifiers on our own pillowcase, then passed it around the table for additions.

On her own pillowcase, Alyona carefully drew a green butterfly and a yellow balloon with a green tree imprinted on it. Next to that was a rainbow with blue, red, yellow, white and black. Overseeing her artistry was a haloed angel with a white face and a red shirt. She painted a smiley face on Alec's and beside it the words: "Dear Alec I love you." Alec's creations combined bright splatters and stripes, overlain with "I love you." And a red fire engine and our dog, Bubba.

"Hugs and kisses all the time, Alyona," read my message to my daughter. I pointed out the three yellow circles to her, each with eyes and a broad grin, and the words, "Love, Mom." How I hoped the picture might comfort her in her dark hours.

We gingerly carried the cases, still drying, to the nurses' station. "Can you guard these with your life, please, until the paint dries?" I asked.

"It would be an honor," a nurse replied.

The Welch family slept well that night.

⌐⌐⌐

Soccer champions score goals and kick the ball the hardest and farthest. The Bridges team did its best in the second skill set. Its games were held on the huge grounds of a Lynchburg school. Often I was the only Bridges family member in the bleachers; some days there might be one or two others. The seats were always packed with the parents of the opposing team's members.

Each Saturday I would bring my folding chair, fully intending to use it. I would choose a spot beside the bleachers from which I could see all the action. Then I'd never sit down.

The reality is that I've never been able to sit still or keep my mouth shut at a sports event, and in the case of Alyona's games, that was doubly true. I ran up and down the sideline after the runner and ball. I hollered continuously—"Great kick," I'd bellow, or "Way to hustle," or "Good Block, Alyona," or "Go Green." Some might call it annoying; I prefer to call it passionate.

Alyona's teammates regarded me with bemused stares. They were unaccustomed to so much attention; so much so, in fact, that they were perplexed as to how to respond, or even what my enthusiasm meant. Some asked Alyona if I was crazy.

"The kids think you are weird," my daughter informed me. "Can you stop the noise?" She'd come to me at halftime of the first game, her head hung low.

"You don't want me to cheer?" I asked, a little hurt.

"Mom," she said, "you're embarrassing me!"

I recalled my stint as a high school student, on the Little Rebels. My parents had never missed a game or practice. As I stood ready for a grounder to be hit to second base, I'd hear my mother's voice boom from the stands: "It's coming your way, Nancy." Or on those exciting double plays that saw me catch a toss from the shortstop, tag second and fire the ball to first, I'd hear, "Great throw!"

Silence on the sideline would be a travesty, I decided. I ignored Alyona's request.

And look: Head bowed, a small, dark-haired boy with penetrating eyes approached me during the second game. "My name's Justin," he said. "Can you shout my name too?" He seemed embarrassed.

"Absolutely," I told him. His eyes lit up.

Not long after, a girl walked up. "Remember Amber, that's me. Yell my name, too, please." Her reddish blond hair matched the fiery spirit I saw in her eyes and in her play on the field.

I added their names to my repertoire, and used them generously during the second half. "Way to go after the ball, Amber," I screamed. "What a great kick, Justin." More children came to see me at the beginning of the third game, and now I had to write their names down on a post-it with shorthand identifiers—red hair, blue shirt, goalie. I realized that, Alyona's reaction aside, The Bridge's players didn't mind my shouting, but were simply baffled by it. They were unaccustomed to such support, unfamiliar with parental pride. They associated a shouted name with anger and imminent punishment.

It got so that players crowded around me at the beginning of each game, to be sure I wrote their names down. Each time one connected with the ball, he glanced my way, waiting to hear his name broadcast more or less to the world. In that moment, everyone knew who he was, and that he'd done good. Regardless of how the team fared—and it never fared well—he felt like a champion.

I have no doubt that I am brimming with self-confidence and a "can-do" spirit because my parents believed in me and were generous in their emotional support. Because of them, I never doubted that I could achieve whatever goals I might set for myself. I vowed that I would always be my children's greatest cheerleader. I vowed that I would never stop believing in them, even when their own self-confidence faltered. I vowed that I would applaud even their smallest successes. Always.

Chapter 15

My brother Ben, a former Marine and Vietnam veteran, has long struggled with the insidious aftereffects of his service. Although he eventually obtained his CPA and a job in the federal government, strict schedules, rules and expectations came to vex him. Ultimately, he went on disability.

At the time he lived in an 800-square foot cabin nestled in the isolated woods of the Shenandoah Mountains, a couple of hours west of Lynchburg. Although he had running water and electricity, he had no phone or TV and few visitors, which suited him fine. But he kept up with the goings-on in civilization, and one day saw ads for dilapidated homes in a deeply depressed section of Lynchburg that was undergoing urban renewal. On a whim, he purchased a home, sight-unseen.

He knew no one in Lynchburg and had only traveled through the city while driving a truck—that, and on visits to my older brother and me when we were students at Lynchburg College. A year prior to Alyona being admitted to The Bridges, he relocated to Lynchburg to work on the place.

The two-story, frame house was located in the heart of the inner city and had been a well-known venue for drug deals. Its neighborhood had a high rate of robbery and murder. Boards were missing from its exterior and half of the window frames were off-kilter, leaving wide gaps between sills and the surrounding walls. Missing floor boards made the simple act of walking from one room to the next a hazardous challenge. Twenty or so pigeons nested in the attic, and via the holes in the ceiling and walls, had access to the entire house. There was no plumbing or electrical power. The ancient heating system had given up the ghost. The basement had a dirt floor. The porch roof sagged dramatically.

Ben, a born handyman, looked at this wreck and envisioned a two-bedroom showplace with a great room and a small but smart kitchen. He built an eight-by-ten-foot, reinforced room on the second floor, invisible from outside the house, protected by a solid door with a security lock. He tapped into a nearby electrical line and ran power into the room. He kept his cot, clothes, tools, equipment, food and a small camp stove in this inner sanctum.

On our first visit to Uncle Ben's, getting inside required a balancing act: The children and I crossed a narrow plank to the front door; Ben had ripped out the rotting porch, leaving a four-foot-deep pit.

Once we'd passed that initial test, Ben laid the day's tasks before us: Two of us were to mix cement and water. The third member of the team would be in the hole with Uncle Ben. Many of the bricks that had supported the porch had crumbled, leaving holes and cracks; the "pit" person scooped a dollop of prepared cement onto a large spatula, which he then held like a painter's palette as he used a smaller spatula like a brush to apply the right amount of cement needed to fill the holes.

At first, we tried to bring an artistry to the task. In time, however, we noticed that Uncle Ben slapped cement into twenty holes for each of our five, and we adopted his style. The process acquired a musical rhythm—scoop, scoop, slap, spread; scoop, scoop, slap, spread.

The reward for a day's labor was Chinese buffet. Because Ben was living sans shower, we rushed to the restroom on arriving at the restaurant, aiming for quick sink baths. A lot of soap and dozens of paper towels later, each of us emerged a bit more presentable for dinner.

A later visit was devoted to destruction. "Choose your weapon," Ben said by way of a greeting. He pointed us to a table crowded with claw hammers and crowbars of various sizes and weights. Once we stood armed and ready, Ben pointed to various inside walls and explained that we'd tear down as many of them as possible, creating fewer but bigger rooms.

On Ben's signal we raised our weapons and commenced the attack, screaming as loud as we could at the same time. It was a gloriously happy, invigorating and therapeutic release, one that particularly appealed to Alyona: On those days when other work was planned but she arrived feeling contrary, we shifted our plans to include some wall-beating. We pounded until the muscles in our arms screamed, raced to see who could remove the most wallboard in the shortest time, traded walls and tools to vary our tasks. We took breaks when we couldn't breathe for all the dust, gulping water as we waited for it to settle. We screamed until our voices stopped working. By the end of the day we were ghostlike, white dust on every hair and in every pore, our clothes infused.

Ben had no gender biases. All of us took our turns using the table saw, circular saw or drill. He was meticulous about safety—he'd plant his hand on the children's as he guided them in adjusting the saw or pushing the wood. All cuts were "very good," although I'm sure he corrected a few when we were out of sight.

Going to Uncle Ben's and working on the house became a highlight of our weekends. Actually, just Ben's company was enough to get the kids excited. He also accompanied us to movies at which we consumed popcorn by the barrel. Play came naturally to him, so he made an excellent counterbalance to my sometimes too-serious ways.

Ben also was immune to public embarrassment, which was a real plus around Alyona. One balmy evening we drove to a restaurant where everyone but Alyona was interested in eating. She was fierce in objecting to our choice. "This is where we are going to eat," I told her on the way, "whether you like it or not." She screamed and kicked at the car's front seats. We ignored her. She screamed louder.

Customers clustered outside the restaurant, enjoying quiet conversation and the oncoming sunset. As we opened the car doors and Alyona's screeches tore into the twilight calm, the talk halted.

I told her she could join us when she got herself under control. With that, Ben, Alec and I strolled past the gawkers, who apparently were too stunned to offer help, call the police or ask questions. As we walked, a cacophony of screams and thuds emanated from my car.

We were seated at a table by the window from which we could observe the car. The restaurant's glass was tinted, enabling us see Alyona while remaining invisible to her. She was tireless. Scraps of paper swirled around inside the station wagon as if caught in a wind tunnel. She clambered over the seats in search of items to hurl or break. Every few minutes the car would rock violently, as she threw herself around the cabin and kicked at the doors.

A couple of times she fell still, and I could see her surveying the parking lot, checking to see if I was on my way. I was savoring delicious Asian salad.

After twenty minutes she emerged from the car soaked, flushed and exhausted. Her every movement telegraphed defeat and anger: the slow but hard stride, the clenched jaw, the hunched shoulders. Without comment she sat down at our table. She announced her selection to the waitress— "hamburger and fries"—without even looking at the menu. After all had eaten, we walked silently to the car. Alyona grudgingly straightened up the mess she'd made, but I felt that there was unfinished business to complete before we returned her to The Bridges. The mood was guarded. Words during dinner had been few and measured, as we took pains to avoid another outburst. We'd made a few genuine attempts at laughter, but Alyona's fit had skewed everything. I didn't want to say goodbye while walking on eggshells.

So when we'd climbed into the car, I tried an experiment. "Remember the primal scream, like we do when knocking down Uncle Ben's walls?" I asked. The children looked at me a bit puzzled, but Ben's eyes twinkled.

"Well," I said, "we're going to sit right here and do some primal screams so we can get out all this negative energy."

"Here in the parking lot?" Alyona and Alec responded in unison.

"Yep," I nodded. "On the count of three. One, two three."

Alyona released a mere whimper. Ben, Alec and I threw back our heads and yelled with all our might. Strolling restaurant patrons again stopped and stared. You could read in their faces a mixture of fear, intrigue and amusement: Should they run, hide, call the police, help us—or just stand back and enjoy the show?

"That wasn't good enough, Alyona." I told her, once we'd run out of breath. She mumbled that she was embarrassed.

Too bad, I told her. "We're going to keep doing it, Alyona, until you're as loud as we are."

Her second try wasn't much better, but on the third, I could hear her high-pitched shriek behind my right ear. She was peering at Alec, determined to be the louder of the two. He stared back. We all reached for the mightiest of screams. God, it was cathartic.

When we finally ran out of strength and lung capacity, we burst into spontaneous laughter. We said goodbye at The Bridges with hugs and kisses and easy barter.

We also spent a lot of time in God's therapy office—which is to say, hiking. Uncle Ben, who had hiked the entire Appalachian Trail, could always be persuaded to join us. Following the red-blazed trees to a mountaintop overlook was hard work with a breathtaking payoff: views that stretched for miles across valleys and lesser ridges.

Whether enjoying the sound of fallen leaves crunching underfoot or inhaling the perfume of spring blossoms, I felt like I was visiting the backwoods for the first time. Butterflies and cardinals were our partners as we hiked, and the children greeted their appearance with glee.

Ah, but Alyona's dark spells could materialize even in the woods. One brisk, overcast day, we set out on a walk up Massanuttan Mountain, a massif in the Shenandoah Valley. Occasional shafts of sun tunneled through the trees and dappled the trail below. It was good hiking weather, and we were well-energized for the adventure. My backpack was stuffed with apples, crackers, water bottles and peanut butter sandwiches. Ben, Alec and I were up for the short four-mile hike and were optimistic that we might spot some deer or rabbits.

But Alyona complained constantly, a worrisome sign. A half-mile into the trek, she refused to go any further and plopped down on a rock. We begged her to go on. She didn't want to hear it. Thinking that she might want to have company in the woods, rather than be by herself, I insisted that the rest of us walk on, and gave Alyona permission to sit at the rock until we returned.

She instead abruptly shifted her strategy: Without warning, she leapt from the rock and tore through the woods, heading straight for the edge of a cliff—and a drop of several hundred feet.

Ben hurried Alec back to the car as I took after her. I hadn't moved that fast since running sprints in high school, but the ground was covered with wet, slippery leaves, so that traction was non-existent, and as the cliff's edge loomed I worried that I wouldn't catch her in time. She drew so close to the precipice that she wouldn't be able to stop from a full gallop. "Please, God, do something!" I prayed.

At that instant, Alyona's right foot seemed to skate over the leaves, her sneaker losing its grip, and she went down hard, sprawling on the damp forest floor. I reached her before she could get up. Half-carrying her, half-pushing, I managed to corral her back to the car. We were both whipped.

Oblivious to how close to danger she had ventured she was angry that we had ignored her little fit. I was relieved we hadn't been killed.

On the way back to The Bridges I calmed myself by remembering an earlier hike I'd made up Grandfather Mountain with Alec. How different it had been from the drama just passed—and how well it showcased the progress Alec had been able to make.

It had been a hot, sunny day with only an occasional wisp of a breeze. I had assured Alec that he could make the climb; with complete trust and confidence he clambered over the rocks at the back of the trail and followed me uphill.

He walked without complaint, even as the day got hotter and the climb steeper. Sweat poured down our faces and we breathed heavily, but he marched on.

"I'll lead, mom," he announced, high up the mountain, and he got us to a thirty-foot slope of a large, jagged stone under a rock overhang. To the trail's left was a thick rope anchored at the top, and knotted at regular intervals along its length. "I'll go first," declared my brave young boy.

Grabbing the rope he pulled himself, one hand over the other, up the slope. "It's easy, mom," he hollered back down to me. "You can do it."

From there, he led the way up a ladder built into a twenty-foot cliff. Each step bolstered his certainty that he would succeed. His pace actually quickened, despite his tired muscles, as we neared the top.

Tall grass waving in the wind welcomed us to the summit. Below lay a lush, green mountain valley speckled with dots of blue, yellow and orange wildflowers. Soaked, we set a place for a picnic on a large flat rock, and tucked into lunch as puffy clouds glided by below us. We had the mountains to ourselves that day. The only voices we heard were our own.

Oh, how I now wished that Alyona could feel even a shade of the delight her brother and I had shared that day.

When Ben traded his truck for an RV, we took up camping. It was a compact vehicle with a sofa bed aft, a double bed over the cab and a dinette that converted to a bed amidship. Alyona and I slept over the cab; Alec got the dinette. The camper had a generator, so we were self-sufficient when it came to lights, heat and refrigeration. Much to the children's delight, a small TV was mounted behind the front passenger seat.

We started modestly, pulling the camper into parking lots frequented by truckers. It might not have qualified, technically, as camping—there were no campfires or S'mores, or trees, for that matter—but the children felt secure with civilization in sight. In place of waking to birdsongs, we heard the revving diesels of neighboring semis.

Braver, we took the camper to national forest campgrounds and to the shore of Smith Mountain Lake. Ben's prowess at building campfires, no matter how wet the wood, bordered on magic, and the family's respect for my culinary skills was bumped up a notch by my mastery of foods skewered on sticks and thrust into the flames. Alyona and Alec enjoyed the combination of outdoor camping and the RV's hominess, security and TV.

A former backpacker, I welcomed the sounds of the night and early morning—the crickets, bird calls and rustle of leaves as animals moved in the dark. Soon the children came to feel the same ease; their moods tended to be tranquil whenever we camped. Camping had become therapeutic.

⌒◡⌒

I grew up during the Vietnam War. Both of my brothers are Marine Corps veterans of the fighting. I recall having talked with returned veterans who were classmates of mine in college. A common thread was the difficulty they'd had rejoining their families; they didn't fit into the family routines established in their absence.

I began to better understand their isolation and frustration as we worked towards Alyona's discharge from The Bridges and her re-integration with the family. Although Alec and I had visited her weekly and called daily, Alyona felt an interloper in her own home.

Alec and I had grown comfortable playing quiet games of double Solitaire and checkers in the evenings. We didn't watch much television. Alyona, meanwhile, had grown accustomed over the past sixteen months to nightly TV. She thrived on being among adolescent girls and engaged in talk about boys, hair, makeup and clothes. She'd lived among rebellion and the frequent use of profanity. She relied on a well-defined schedule for meals, therapy appointments, entertainment, laundry, showers. Staffers were on duty to respond to her emotional needs 24/7. She'd come to depend on a system that measured her behavior in black-and-white, numerical terms—and which decided whether she'd get to attend social events, movies, travel to a local college basketball game. Her world at The Bridges was simple, predictable. I knew that our life at home could never be this well-regimented. The only hard-and-fast routine I'd observed with Alec was getting to school on time.

And I had come to relax with just Alec in the house. He and I knew each other's nuances and could laugh at ourselves. Some days he intentionally wore his shirts inside-out and backwards, or selected unmatched socks or wore his shoes on the wrong feet, and insisted, over my laughing objections, that he be allowed to leave the house like that. School often called, asking: "Did you know that Alec had his shirt on backwards today?"

"Yes," I'd say, "but he was excited about going to school."

I felt confident setting boundaries and consequences for him. I didn't fear his reactions. I feared Alyona's. I worried how to create an environment suitable for such divergent behaviors——intense and structured versus laid-back and adaptable.

It was standing room only in the school cafeteria on the night of the Christmas pageant and Alec's solo. Twenty-five first graders dressed in their finest stood nervously on stage, the girls tugging at new and scratchy dresses, the boys with ties and tight collars.

My heart skipped a few beats as Alec walked to the microphone, waited for the signal to begin, and opened his mouth on cue.

"Oh, come little children, oh come, one and all," he sang in little-boy soprano. "While angels are singing sweet songs from above." He calmly completed verse after verse from memory. Most in the audience knew his story. Other than a few sniffles, including my own, there was complete silence; only his voice wafted through the room. A few mothers glanced my way, offering soft smiles or a nod of acknowledgement.

This was a boy who not long before had to be carried kicking and screaming to his class. Who'd made a war zone of his bedroom. Who'd punched me, pulled my hair, clawed at my eyes. I welcomed his transformation; I also feared his tranquility would be threatened when Alyona returned home. And I had no clue how to avoid it.

In preparation for Alyona's return, she was granted weekend passes which were often spent at my brother's in North Carolina, camping with Ben or a most-telling time when we attended the marriage of Ms. Jones, the first-grade teacher in whose class Alyona had had the meltdown that led to her commitment.

She'd visited Alyona several times at The Bridges, and had invited both Alyona and Alec to help hand out favors at the wedding. Alyona was thrilled at the prospect and felt very important. More to the point, she felt normal, as one with the other children who were helping.

The Outer Banks bed and breakfast at which the ceremony took place was newly redecorated and tall enough to offer a sweeping view of the Atlantic. It was a weathered, two-story beach house, wrapped in porches, furnished in wicker and rope hammocks, sweet william and crepe myrtle blooming purple and red along its front path.

Alyona looked lovely in a white, short-sleeved cotton dress with lace and pin tucks on the bodice. Her long brown hair glistened. She was the picture of politeness and poise as she handed a little silver bell to each arriving guest.

Alec wore a white, short-sleeved dress shirt, slate blue pants and a blue paisley tie. I was taken by the effect that being dressed up had on him: He stood taller, walked more confidently, and used "sir" and "ma'am" when speaking to adults.

To see their easy sociability brought me pride and hope. They were joyful, animated and quick to follow instructions. They frequently asked if there was anything else they could do to help. They spoke readily with Ms. Jones' parents and other adults. I had been a bit hesitant to have them participate, as I was unsure of how they would act—especially Alyona. Ms. Jones had assured me that they'd be fine. She had been right.

The wedding was conducted in the living room, before windows overlooking the ocean. The sun bathed the entire room. At the end of the ceremony, a simple sentence reminded me of the challenge that lay ahead. As the bride and groom turned toward us after exchanging their vows, the minister announced: "I present to you Mr. and Mrs. Morgan."

Alyona reacted instantly. "You're not Mrs. Morgan," she blurted. "You're Ms. Jones, my teacher!"

Everyone chuckled, viewing the comment as the innocent words of a child. I knew better. It was a demonstration of Alyona's deeply seated need for constancy. It was her desperate entreaty that nothing change. She feared the new.

It required her to adapt, to test her flexibility, to devise solutions. The world away from the structured and constant Bridges was a frightening place for her. She was about to re-enter it.

PART IV

New Beginning

Chapter 16

I learned to be grateful. After twenty months at The Bridges Alyona was back home, not cured but certainly better. And over time, I had grown more accepting of her limits, better able to revel in small victories rather than agitate over missteps. I tried to find any tidbit of progress—cursed less, anger lasted a shorter amount of time, caused no harm, didn't try to engage Alec in the fray, apologized. I lowered my expectations and vigorously praised small achievements. I tried to take nothing for granted.

Sometimes, though, it helped to have a push toward this enlightened attitude. Example: A sleepover at a school-mate's house. Alyona, and two friends, Betty and Mary, had known each other since first grade and shared many of the same classes. Alyona and Betty were both strong-willed and liked to be in charge. They spent a lot of time together, though after a couple hours, Alyona and Betty. would usually require physical separation. Neither held back.

One weekend, Alyona proposed that she be able to sleep over at Mary's; Betty would also be there. "Mom, we'll be fine," Alyona assured me. "Mary has lots of games we can play at her house."

"I have lots of food. How bad can they be if I keep feeding them?" Mary's mother asked me. "They've never had a sleep-over. Let's give it a try."

Betty's mother and I agreed to it, but we were sure to leave our home and cell numbers. I was not optimistic.

Two hours passed and no phone call. Four hours and still no call. Maybe I was wrong, I thought. Maybe this will work. Maybe Alyona really is learning to work out differences in a calmer way. Six hours and no call—this was a record of calm between Alyona and Betty.

The feared call came at midnight, eight hours into the sleep-over. "Betty and Alyona are at it," the desperate voice on the other end said. "Yelling at each other, pulling hair and throwing everything. Please come get Alyona." I could hear shouts and thuds in the background.

Betty's mother and I arrived at the same time and she chuckled as we walked up the sidewalk: "Well, it's a record for them." I had been prepared to admonish Alyona for fighting, but her words reminded me to appreciate even small steps forward.

"Hey guys, you played together nicely for the longest time you've ever done," I said on seeing the girls. "Way to go." With that, Alyona's face morphed from an angry scowl to a smile. A potential meltdown had been averted; we both walked to the car proud of her accomplishment.

In the first weeks after Alyona came home, I looked forward to a nightly ritual: Glass of red wine on my back porch, where I might enjoy a cool lake breeze and a quiet conversation. My companion wore his eyeglasses slightly askew on his elongated nose, and had a professorial, sagacious air.

"So, King," I'd sigh, "how could I have handled it better today?"

I've always been grateful that an artistic friend whimsically added glasses to the shark on the stained-glass porch window she created for me. I could tell that shark anything. He was always a patient listener, and helped me summon fortitude, understanding and resolution, which otherwise eluded me on the most trying of days.

Home life was proving too quiet for Alyona. She was agitated and nervous. It was as if she was afraid that her very own life's energy would be sapped from her body should she relax, even for a moment. The board games and puzzles that Alec and I had come to enjoy bored and frustrated her.

"Let's play Connect Four," Alec invited her.

"No!" she barked back.

Yet she was also frightened by her own history. She lacked trust in her own self-control. The absence of scheduled activities and close supervision was disconcerting to her, frightening, precarious. Home at last after nearly two years away, she frequently voiced yearnings for The Bridges. "I like the point system," she told me. "Why can't you do that?"

"I'm bored," she told me. "We always did something at night at The Bridges."

She wanted to know the exact time we'd do something and how long it would take. She wanted to know the consequences, good and bad, for every choice she made. She wanted to know the specific details of every rule, every boundary and every acceptable variation. She wanted nothing left to her imagination.

If I said she couldn't have or do something, then she wanted to know how long that would remain true. We used oven timers, microwave timers and egg timers. She would hold a timer in her hand or stand and stare at the microwave timer until the buzzer sounded. She preferred the microwave timer as it counted seconds as well as minutes.

She was a tenacious negotiator, always trying to reshape the boundaries of a rule or routine. This was an effort aimed less at making things easier than at better controlling her behavior. Vagary offered opportunities for failure, and she truly wanted to succeed.

"If I go to my room right now and also clean it," she asked me, "can I watch TV tonight so I don't have to wait until tomorrow night?"

"If I do your laundry and mine, can we still go to the movies?"

"You said no TV for two days. So does that mean I can start watching TV in two days in the morning? Or at night?"

There was little spontaneity or joy about her. All was calculation. She was constantly assembling a daily blueprint for acceptable behavior.

Although she showed tremendous improvement, the effort was taking its toll. She was visibly tense. She struggled to conform to the quiet of the house, and to honor what she perceived to be an expectation that she never be angry or confrontational.

"I didn't get angry today," she'd boast at night, when I knew the truth was that she hadn't reacted badly when she was, in fact, angry at me for not taking them to the movies.

"Alyona, it's OK to be angry," I tried to explain to her. "Even pouting is OK. You could have even stomped your feet and walked away and that would be OK. You were upset because I wouldn't let you have something that you wanted, and that's normal. I'm proud of you for not having a fit."

I succeeded mostly in confusing her. In her mind, anger was the enemy. If she could avoid anger then life would be copasetic. This internal strife was building. An explosion was coming.

It came two months after she left The Bridges, during one of her therapy sessions. Alyona had been in the office about fifteen minutes while I contented myself reading Newsweek. It was quiet. A small boy sat on the floor playing with building blocks while his mother read a fashion magazine. The waiting room was painted a calming shade of blue and the sliding windows giving access to the office staff were closed. I welcomed an hour of uninterrupted reading.

Suddenly, the door to the offices flew open and Alyona's therapist burst into the room, her hair mussed and cheeks flushed. "Alyona's tearing up the office," she cried. "She's uncontrollable. I'm calling the rescue squad and the police for an emergency admission."

My heart rate and adrenaline spiked. Tossing the Newsweek aside, I raced past the therapist and into her office. Alyona looked and sounded more like an animal than a nine-year-old girl. She was shrieking loathsome epithets and hurling at the wall any item she could grab from the shelves. Her face was contorted with rage. Her eyes blazed.

As I walked further into the room, a colorful ceramic clown just missed my head. "Alyona," I said, "stop."

"You motherfucker," she bellowed. She fast-balled a stuffed animal at me, then dashed at me, swinging her fists. Her eyes were glassed-over, her pupils large; I wasn't sure that she even recognized me. I planted my feet and braced for impact.

Her fists came first; as I blocked them, she kicked and kneed me. She broke away to latch onto the bookcase, and pulled until it started to tip away from the wall. I grabbed her from behind, lost my balance, and we both went flailing to the floor, along with books, dolls and toys that fell from the teetering shelves. I rolled us away just as the bookcase came crashing down, one corner slamming into a chair with a heavy thud; had it not been for the chair, the pine case would have landed on our legs.

"Alyona," I grunted as I tried to pin her arms, "what's wrong? Talk to me."

She didn't hear me. She didn't see me. She pulled my hair and bit at any part of my body that came within range. We rolled around like two fifth-grade boys. She seemed possessed, driven to purge herself of anything inside. As if she sought for emptiness.

She had grown bigger and stronger during her tenure at The Bridges, and as we struggled I realized that she'd become much more difficult to handle. When she broke away from my grasp, she immediately pounced on me and unleashed a salvo of books or knick-knacks.

I had no idea what had brought this on. She had not had any problems during the week. When we'd arrived at the therapist, Alyona had been cheery, laughing. She'd shown off a drawing she'd made: a green field, a big, leafy tree, a gang of flowers; she had carefully drawn five or six petals and a yellow center on each of the blossoms. A happy picture. No indication of a pending meltdown.

I now realized that the past couple of months of apparent calm had been a façade. She'd been masking a seething rage—or, perhaps more accurately, a seething fear.

Her emotions were her albatross. In her heart they made her unworthy of love, kindness, even family—and they made life oddly simple. She knew how to deal with the repercussions of anger, but not those of love.

By the time the ambulance and police arrived, Alyona was totally spent. She offered no resistance to being placed on the gurney. Her eyes were glazed over. Her fury was gone, replaced by a dazed confusion. She seemed unaware of where she was or even who she was.

"What's your name, hon?" an EMT asked her.

Alyona just stared. She was baffled. Her hand was limp in mine. "Your name is Alyona," I told her, my heart aching. I added: "I love you very much."

"We have to strap her down, just to be sure," the EMT told us, "but we won't make it real tight." A policeman told me we'd head straight for the hospital, which was expecting us.

I, too, was confused and frightened. I had never before required the assistance of police, and I had only ridden in an ambulance as a pediatric resident transporting sick children. I was no longer a doctor, in charge and in control; I was the mother of a patient, reliant on strangers, helpless. I felt mindless, vulnerable and compliant.

I climbed into the ambulance beside Alyona, stroked her hair, and tried to comfort and reassure her with my eyes. She had reverted to a scared little girl, clinging tightly to my hand. "I'm sorry, mommy, I'm sorry," she said softly.

"I know, Alyona," I whispered to her. "It's all right. I'm not angry."

We arrived to the locked ward of the hospital and two nurses let us in. I was a bystander as the EMT briefed the staff and a nurse welcomed Alyona, sounding more like a concierge, "You'll like it here, Alyona," she said. "We have lots of activities and the therapists and doctors are very nice."

After the preliminaries, a nurse turned to me, "Can you tell us some of the history," she said, "and what medicines she takes." The information flowed out of me in rote fashion, requiring little thought. I had shared Alyona's history many times—to school, doctors and therapists. While I was talking, I glanced around the large, open room that seemed to serve as both living room and dining area. We were standing beside a wooden dining table where an adult and a pre-teen boy were playing checkers. An older boy and girl, seated on the cargo sofas, were watching a day-time soap on TV, but seemed disengaged from the show. Another boy sat in a chair by the wall, head leaning on his bent arm, staring into space. None paid any mind to Alyona; new admissions were commonplace.

"What do you think brought on this episode?" the nurse asked.

"I don't know," I sighed, "It started in the therapist's office."

They began to roll her, still on the gurney, back to her room, and I flashed back to leaving her at The Bridges. Sedated, Alyona wasn't screaming as she had then, but my sorrow was just as heavy. And this time, Alec wasn't with me; I felt even more alone and helpless. I swallowed hard and turned back to the nurse. "The doctor will call you," she said. "You will also want to arrange an appointment with the therapist after she has talked with Alyona."

"Yes, I will," I mumbled. "Thanks." I wasn't even sure what she'd said. I stood there for a long time; I didn't want to move. I felt the nurse's hand on my shoulder, steering me towards the door. "This card has all the numbers you'll need," she said, as she handed me a business card. "Call us tomorrow afternoon."

I stepped outside the ward; the door closed and the lock sounded like thunder. I turned in a complete circle, with no place to go. I didn't even have my car; it was back at the therapist's office. I had never felt so lost. I called my friend Pat.

"The therapist may have gotten too close to Alyona's past," the hospital counselor explained, "and Alyona has thick walls protecting her from what must have been a very scary and frightening experience."

"She's not ready to remember," she continued, "and she may never be ready."

"Can she get better without remembering?" I asked.

"Absolutely," she said without hesitation, "but either way, she still has a long ways to go."

"I thought she'd be better after The Bridges," I moaned.

"Nancy, she'll most likely still struggle with some things as an adult," the counselor gently reminded me. "Healing may be a lifetime process."

"I can tell you, though," she added, her tone optimistic, "Alyona has amazing insights for a young child, and that will be a real benefit for her as she gets older. Some may be natural, but I imagine a lot grew from the therapy sessions at The Bridges."

"What can I do to help?" I asked. "I can't just watch her suffer and do nothing."

"You are already doing a lot by being there for her, no matter what," she reassured me. "Alyona is beginning to trust you, but it is scary for her. Give her time, and understand that there will most likely be many more episodes. When Alyona takes several steps forward and it gets too frightening, the meltdown is her retreat."

After five days, Alyona's medications had been adjusted, her emotional status stable and she was ready for discharge. The counselor ordered that I obtain in-home therapy. My first mental impulse was to reject it; it seemed too invasive into my personal life, and an insult, to boot. "You can't do this by yourself," the counselor insisted. "You will be glad you have this resource and support." Looking at Alyona sitting beside me, my hesitation was brief. "Yes," I agreed, "whatever is needed to help Alyona get better."

Her first night home, after she was asleep, I sat before the King on the porch and made myself and Alyona a promise. "You will never go back to that dark memory again unless and until you are ready," I said. "We don't need to know about what happened. Love and the desire to help you heal are far more important than idle curiosity. I only care that you are hurting to a depth with which I can never identify. I know you are afraid of yourself and life. I know you are one of the bravest people I know. I know you can be very funny, observant and bright. I know you have been entrusted to my care, and I will not betray that trust. I know that I want to pick you up in my arms, hug you and make all the bad things disappear. I so wish that it were that easy. I know that you need me. Right now, I may be the only person or thing in whom you believe. I will always be there for you." Amen.

Chapter 17

"We're attached at the hip," is how Judy, the in-home therapist had described the relationship between the two of us. "Twenty-four-seven, call anytime, and I'll be here." She held up her cell phone to emphasize the point. "This is with me at all times; I keep it on and by my bed at night." She explained that, as a licensed therapist, she was to step in early when Alyona was struggling so that she might calm Alyona down, or advise me of some interventions that might stave off a meltdown. She would make regular visits to monitor Alyona's behavior and teach her better ways to handle her frustration and anger. "If talking on the phone doesn't work," she reminded me, "I can be here in twenty minutes, no matter the time of day or night." I wasn't used to such availability of assistance; I don't even call my private physician in the middle of the night. But I had no doubt that Judy meant what she said.

This plucky, mid-thirties woman was intimidated neither by Alyona's aggression nor her declaration, "I don't like you and don't want to talk to you." Judy never raised her voice, but spoke firmly while looking you straight in the eyes.

"You don't need to like me, Alyona," Judy said, "but I will be here when you have problems, and we will work through them together."

"I'm also here for your mom and Alec," she added, "I'm here for the whole family."

Judy never reneged on her promises. She had a keen ability to perceive the underlying issue to Alyona's rage, regardless of the words Alyona was using to express it. This proved invaluable in putting the situation into the right perspective. She also was pregnant and due in six months, which I reckoned would be her tenure with us.

I had expected miracles, I suppose, following Alyona's twenty months at The Bridges. Like the hospital therapist, Judy reassured me that rather than a setback, her explosion at the therapist's office reflected the skin-shedding necessary for her to reach the next level of stability. "She's behaving as we would expect in order to move forward," Judy told me. "Don't be discouraged."

Alyona had achieved a certain comfort at The Bridges. Boundaries, expectations and consequences had been strictly defined and enforced. Her days there presented no deviations; life was a constant, reliable algorithm. Alas: It was impossible to maintain that same predictable style at home. Alyona was being asked to be resilient and discerning, and she felt untethered. Like a blind person, Judy said, she needed to bump against the perimeters and obstacles of her new existence before she could learn to navigate it. In the process, her self-confidence had vanished; she'd grown frantic in her struggle to clarify her surroundings. "She made great strides at The Bridges," Judy said. "We will build on that foundation."

Judy reminded me that Alyona wanted to again experience and enjoy the trust and comfort she had achieved at The Bridges. Yet her behavior so often seemed totally at odds with a desire for normalcy. I believed Judy, but I had great difficulty reconciling her words and Alyona's behaviors.

"She'll have more setbacks," Judy promised, making it sound almost like a good thing. "That's why I'm here."

At times I had to remind myself that it was fear, not hostility, that prompted Alyona's disruptive fits, her aggressive responses; it was easy to forget in the midst of struggle. How was I to feel empathy when her teeth were breaking the skin on my arms, or she had a fistful of my hair? How could fear produce such violence?

It all seemed so counterintuitive to my logical and orderly doctor's mind—seemed, in fact, evidence that God must have a wicked sense of humor. The subject I disliked most in medical school was psychiatry, because it all seemed so nebulous and immeasurable. I had little respect for its theories and what I saw as ambivalent therapeutic interventions. The world was well-defined, to my naïve mind: you simply gathered evidence, used it to determine a course of action, and followed through. I had no real concept of the confusions and distortions that can hijack one's mind and emotions. Through Judy, I was now intently revisiting Psychiatry 101. And I was far more receptive to learning.

<hr>

"Alyona, put the chair down," Eric Heimer said, as she prepared to throw it across the classroom. Alyona was enrolled in a public school in the special education class for children with behavioral problems—"E.D." for short, for emotionally disturbed. Mr. Heimer, the soft-spoken teacher, was able to command attention in a wonderfully gentle manner. He was explicit about his expectations, and the students respected him; he was a teacher they didn't want to disappoint.

But on this day, Alyona didn't mind disappointing. The floor was strewn with paper and loose pencils. Overturned chairs and tables were jumbled in heaps.

"It's not fair," Alyona cried. "I just wanted to talk with Barbara."

Ms. Weaver, the teacher's aide, held out her hand. "Come here and we can sit and draw," she said.

"No," Alyona roared back. "I hate you." She flung a math book at her.

Ms. Weaver hustled Alyona's classmates into the hall as Mr. Heimer put in a call for the principal.

Principal Colleen Leary could hear Alyona screaming during the brief conversation. As she left her office, she grabbed a fashion magazine she knew to be one of Alyona's favorites. Ms. Leary knew all the students in her school, not only by name but also by interest. She might ask a child about his dog, soccer team or new baby sister. She knew Alyona loved to pore over the clothes and hair styles in the magazine.

Several times in the past Alyona had been brought to Ms. Leary's large, carpeted office to answer for her contentious behavior. Ms. Leary and Alyona would sit at two of the chairs around her conference table and flip through Seventeen or Vogue, Ms. Leary commenting on the importance of controlling one's behavior, as only with such control could Alyona hope to look as pretty and happy as the fashion models. Subtle and non-threatening instruction, indeed—and well-received by Alyona.

Ms. Leary arrived in the classroom to find Alyona balled up under a short-legged table at its center; she'd had to origami herself into the tight space and refused to come out.

The principal dropped to her hands and knees. "This is your favorite magazine, Alyona," she said. "Come on out and we can look at the pictures." She turned the pages, pointing out interesting styles.

"No," Alyona snarled. "You come here." Ms. Leary twisted her five-foot-two frame under the table and slid beside Alyona.

I arrived to the two of them discussing which hairdos would look best on each of them, and why. There was no giddiness in Alyona's tone, no anger, not even a trace of the tirade or whatever had prompted it. She seemed content, and practically aglow with Ms. Leary's attention. She welcomed me with a big grin.

While at The Bridges the main focus, rightfully so, had been to make the children's behavior more manageable, predictable and appropriate. When Alyona came home, I had elected to enroll her in her age-appropriate grade level, despite her having fallen substantially behind her classmates. When I'd discussed the matter with her, she'd insisted on remaining two grades ahead of Alec, whom I'd held back; and she liked the option that, with good behavior, she was allowed to join a regular third-grade class, accompanied by Ms. Weaver.

If she applied herself, I felt, she'd be fine—she was quite intelligent, as she'd shown for years: She'd become fluent in English, with no accent, in nine months. I'd drive somewhere once, and she could remember how to replicate the journey. She could play back a conversation from months before, word for word, inflection for inflection. She had an almost photographic awareness of her surroundings, and a preternatural insight into the behavior of others. Besides, she physically looked her age. I decided that I could more easily compensate for her educational shortcomings by way of tutors than manage her hostility and depression at being held back.

It had not gone perfectly. She did poorly on tests and her reading skills lagged. She felt inadequate and stupid. Always a perfectionist, Alyona could not accept her own incompetence. It was easier for her to justify her own misbehavior; that was within her control, and did not speak to any innate deficiency. So a pattern quickly emerged: If she didn't understand something, she'd throw her books or yell at the teacher.

"She's very smart," Mr. Heimer told me. "She just doesn't believe it yet." But, he added, Alyona knew "how to succeed at being bad without working too hard." When Alyona threw a tantrum, he would sit with her one-on-one or allow her to snuggle into a beanbag chair to read aloud, whether to herself or one of the teachers.

Judy met with the teachers to help ensure that Alyona got consistent messages and expectations at school and home. Those conversations helped us all learn to recognize the subtle and not-so-subtle mannerisms that portended Alyona's blow-ups.

For example: Her voice would become toddler-like and squeaky, and she would bounce around the room in a giddy fashion. The teachers tried to refocus her, and thus to avert an eruption; she might respond to some one-on-one time with an adult.

At times this delirious behavior came without warning. At others, it would be an obvious response to a lack of attention: another child might be receiving more time or focus, when Alyona wanted to be at the center; she might simply not want to do her classwork, and a fit seemed a handy way to avoid it. Whatever the case, underlying her behavior was a desire for more control.

In spite of her teachers' intervention, on a good many occasions, Alyona's meltdowns proved unavoidable. She would scream, curse, throw chairs and papers and try to hit her classmates or teachers with books, pencils, crayons. In the wake of some of Alyona's fits, she'd go back to her regular school activities, exhausted and compliant.

Other times, I would pick her up from school and bring her to my office. Often she was subdued and contrite, and would work for hours without complaint. My assistant would be her supervisor and assigned her extensive filing, as if Alyona was one of our volunteers. The more repetitive the task, the more appealing it seemed to be to Alyona.

"Do I get breaks and for how long?" she asked. "What time is my lunch and for how long?" Her retreat back into a regulated, controlled and mundane existence was a necessary part of her recovery. It seemed to re-center her spirit, to provide the down-time her psyche needed to heal.

After-school care was a difficult challenge. Looking for a structured environment, I enrolled both children in a Taekwondo program. This was probably very short-sighted on my part. The expectations and rules were well-defined and strict, so severe and non-flexible that in some ways the class must have mimicked the orphanage.

"Sit straight. Be quiet unless spoken to. Do you want to stand in the corner?" The stern female head of the program, a French woman, also was reminiscent of the caretakers in Odessa.

The program comprised fifty children. Alec's and Alyona's feral instincts returned to the fore. The rules and staff simply became targets for defiance. They were constantly in trouble—behaving disrespectfully, cursing and refusing to follow the rules. Alyona was most often the instigator, but Alec would always join in to defend her. They refused to do the exercises and dared the staff to punish them.

Their punishment—sitting in the classroom, rather than participating in the Taekwondo exercises—seemed more a reward to them. They became more audacious. They refused to do the homework, sassed the staff, attempted to leave the building. They threw their books and papers and tried to hit the administrator. They dared her to hit back.

Eventually, a phone call came. "Come get your kids," the French woman said, "They are hellions and we don't want them in our program anymore."

I made the mistake of attributing the children's bad behavior to a personality conflict with the woman, focusing on her similarity to the orphanage staff. It didn't occur to me that the environment itself was the problem.

I then proceeded to make things worse. Focusing on Alyona's need for structure, I enrolled them in a second Taekwondo program. There, Alyona and Alec became a rambunctious, bullying team. They taunted the staff and other children, striving to pit one against another. They refused to participate in the classes and ran wild through the facility. They would bite, hit and kick any staff member who attempted to constrain them. They had regressed to the querulous, manipulative urchins of their past.

And they were skilled and experienced in that role. The softening of their facial expressions even disappeared, along with their sense of remorse. It was not until then that I saw my mistake. I promised them that I would never enroll them in a similar program.

Setbacks were invited by more than Taekwondo. With the slightest provocation, Alyona would burst into a vengeful and destructive rage at home. She'd throw lamps, chairs and books, upend tables and heavier furniture. She'd refuse to go to her room for time-out or to stop her misbehavior. I locked her in her room for everyone's safety.

Not without a fight, however.

"Alec, help me," she'd shout to her brother. "Push mommy away." He'd try to tug me away from her. If I went to call Judy, Alyona would grab for the phone, slug me or push me against the wall. One of us would have a nose bleed by the time I got her upstairs. Since she had broken her lock, I would quickly slam the door after pushing her into her room and then have to throw all my weight against it to keep it shut.

Once Alyona was in her room, Alec's allegiance changed. He scrambled to help me, to find the cell phone and dial Judy's number. Most of the time, she recommended that we call 911 and promised that she was on her way, regardless of whether it was nine in the evening or one in the morning.

By the time the police arrived, Alyona was exhausted and quiet, but the destruction would be readily apparent—rooms in shambles, floors littered with broken lamps and sofa cushions and chairs overturned. Alyona would only occasionally respond to the police officer's questions and then with only a yes or no.

Judy would hurry to explain the situation. "Alyona has a history of violence," she'd say. "She was recently discharged from Maryview Psychiatric unit. I can stay to be sure everything is OK."

The police responded with a battery of questions. "Do you want to press charges? Do you feel you are in danger? Do you want us to do an emergency admission?"

I hugged Alec, who clung by my side. At such moments, I felt a visitor in someone else's life. All my education and public health experience were of no help to me—or, it seemed to Alyona. I had no words.

"Alyona is calmer now, so I don't believe she is a threat," Judy would say. "If it's OK with you, officers, I'll stay awhile and help Dr. Welch decide what she wants to do." I'd numbly nod assent.

Judy was there for my legal protection, as well as my physical well-being: Her presence and knowledge of the situation dispelled any suspicions the police might entertain regarding child abuse—which, given the tumultuous surroundings and the child locked in her room, they might well have had.

At bed time, as I stood in Alyona's room, amid the debris and broken sheetrock, Alyona's "I love you, mommy" seemed a cruel joke.

Judy, more pragmatic than consoling, was not one to waste words. "We need a plan," she said. "This will happen again and safety is the first concern. Alyona will get better with therapy and time but we have to protect you and Alec in the meantime."

She outlined what needed to happen. "Take everything out of Alyona's room except for the mattress," she instructed. "Make arrangements with neighbors for safe houses for Alec so he can go there anytime of day or night and be taken in. Send Alec to a safe house as soon as Alyona erupts.

"Call me sooner so perhaps I can talk Alyona down," she said. "Know that we will not hesitate to call 911 or press charges if need be."

I cringed at the thought. Judy explained to me that sometimes the best thing to do is charge the child with assault or destruction of property. Appearing before the judge and having to abide by legally imposed sentences makes a lasting impression. It lets the child know that the parent's standards are supported by the law; and breaking them results in enforceable consequences. She reassured me that usually, for a first offense, the sentence is probation and community service and, with good behavior, it may be removed from the record. Still, the thought of charging my own child didn't set right with me.

Over the next few months, six of Alyona's explosions achieved a state of actual combat, and five ended with emergency admissions to the hospital. The only common denominator was that not getting her way usually came first.

One evening, she didn't like the dinner I'd prepared and I refused to change the menu to suit her. She threw her plate of food on the floor and refused to clean it up. When I insisted, she went ballistic. She threw anything she could lay her hands on—plates, knick-knacks from the shelves, the dog's water bowl, placemats, pillows from the sofa, lamps, books—-aiming most of them directly at me. I ducked and dodged but her speed and agility were far superior to mine, so while I avoided getting hurt, I couldn't grab her to stop the attack.

Alec, frightened, tried to stop the much bigger and stronger Alyona. She shoved him out of her way. "Go to a safe house, Alec," I hollered. "Go, Go. I'll be all right."

My scrawny little boy was determined to be the protector and to insert himself between us. His fearlessness made me fear for his safety all the more.

I was trying to shoo him out of the house when Alyona gave me a shove on the stairs and I fell backwards, slamming hard on four steps before thudding against the wall on the landing. I was lying with my feet uphill of my head, but more startled than hurt. "Alec, call 911," I shouted.

"Come quick," I heard him tell the operator. "My sister pushed my mom down the stairs." He recited our address.

"Hang up now and punch in Judy's quick-dial number," I told him. "Then give me the phone and go to a safe house."

Now Alyona went after Alec for helping me. I separated the two, and Alec darted out of the house. Judy answered the phone. She could hear the cacophony of shouts and door slams, as I held the phone over my head and out of Alyona's reach. She punished me by kicking hard against my shins.

I asked Alyona several times to speak with Judy. When she finally did, the counselor convinced her to go to her room. But, even in her room, Alyona's rage continued. I held the bedroom door shut while Judy and the police hurried to the scene, the sounds of pandemonium clear on the other side.

By the time help arrived, Alyona was literally crawling through the splintered bottom half of the door. It wasn't the only time she did such damage; once she pushed her way clear through a wall and into my bedroom. This time, at Judy's behest, Alyona was admitted to a psychiatric unit for a couple days to calm down and to have her medications adjusted.

As Alyona wrestled with her fears and fits, I had my own struggles against meltdowns, some successful, some not. Frazzled, exhausted, I sometimes kept my temper only by forcing myself to do what Alyona had been taught to do at The Bridges: by considering the consequences.

Exhibit A: My friend, Theresa, was over one night. She's short but long on spunk, jovial, quick to find a positive twist in even the most dire of circumstances. From their first meeting, Alec and Alyona loved her spontaneity and playfulness. She was no pushover, mind you; she also set clear rules and, for the most part, the children would abide by them. She once watched Alyona and Alec for five days during a hurricane and its aftermath, without electricity, while my professional obligations required that I be elsewhere. I arrived home to all smiles.

Anyway, she was visiting for dinner, and while washing the dishes after the meal, I became aware of hissing sounds in the living room. After each hiss, Alyona and Alec would shriek with laughter.

"What's going on?" I hollered.

There was no answer, just whispers and shushing.

I tiptoed towards the room fully prepared to catch them in the act of some misdeed, though I didn't know what. It had been a troublesome day and I was in no mood for shenanigans.

I was shocked by what I saw—-and at this point, that's saying something. They were both covered from head-to-toe in shaving cream and rolling around on the sofa, which was equally coated in the stuff. Alyona had planned to use shaving cream and food dye to make greeting cards with colorful, marble-patterned covers and we'd gone to the store and purchased several cans earlier in the day. One empty can was on the floor and four more were on the table.

"What are you doing?" I shouted. "You're a mess and so is the furniture!" White was smeared all over their faces. They had pressed shaving cream into every crevice of their clothes. Both had shaving-cream hand prints on their chests. Alyona had "earrings" of white foam. Alec had massaged the shaving cream into his hair, then sculpted it into a towering spire. Even as I yelled, each child continued to spray the other, along with the sofa and the carpet.

I could feel the rage billowing inside me. My cheeks flushed. My muscles tensed. How could they be so disrespectful and destructive, and think that it was funny? They knew better.

"Noooooo," was all I got out, before Theresa suddenly sprang from hiding, hollering, "Take that!" Before I'd even registered her presence, she aimed a can straight at my face and hair. I saw her wink at the kids.

I was too stunned to speak or move. What did she think she was doing? Whose side was she on? How could she be complicit in this blatant act of disrespect, in my home and with my children? Was I the only adult in the room? The only one with some sense of right and wrong?

There she stood, laughing and grinning right along with the kids, while shaving cream dripped from my face onto the floor. Was I missing something here? My basic concept of parental authority was turned upside down. If I screamed at the kids, I would also have to scream at Theresa. That would be demeaning for both of us, and make it harder for her when she watched them in the future. At the same time, I felt demeaned. How was I to save face here? If I vented my anger, Alyona most likely would overreact, storm out of the room, or worse, start fighting. And for what? What was their real infraction? The shaving cream was easy to clean up; after all it wasn't sticky whipped topping or paint. In the grand scheme of things, what was the matter??

Would it be worth risking a meltdown to exercise my authority? And in the chaos that would follow would anyone remember the fun he or she had been having? And if I staunchly demanded that they stop, what would I be saying to them—that spontaneity wasn't permitted, even if it wasn't harmful? That they shouldn't be flexible, should always do everything my way because I was the boss?

If I was seeking order, risking a meltdown certainly wouldn't get it. And maybe running around laughing and spraying shaving cream wasn't without order; maybe a group clean-up afterwards could be enormously reaffirming.

My head was filled with a whirlwind of conflicting ideas and thoughts on a course of action. Surely control and authority weren't worth sacrificing a joyous, memorable family time over, especially when no damage had been done that couldn't be cleaned. The more I thought about it—and bear in mind, all this thinking was compressed into something less than two seconds—the less an affront it all seemed, and the more like fun. I had encouraged these kids to do crazier things before—like screaming at the top of our lungs in a car parked outside a crowded restaurant.

I grabbed a can.

The children didn't hesitate. They left no part of my body uncovered. I felt like cake being frosted. I got in some good shots, myself, and the three of them went after each other with great gusto and roars of laughter.

Soon we were chasing each other around the kitchen, spraying and slipping on the wet floor. We laughed until tears made streams in the white froth on our faces and we could no longer stand.

As we cleaned the mess, we compared notes of who'd managed the best shots and reveled in the shapes we'd made with our moistened hair. I marveled, as we scooped foam from the sofa, that we'd turned a potential volcano into a few minutes of pure fun. The lesson I'd learned would save many a later day, when I could remember to pause a moment, think things through and re-set the tone.

At other times, though, I became tense and far too quick to react. All vestiges of patience were dissipated. I expected the worst, rather than building on the positive. Professionally a model of the calm, unruffled approach to crisis, at home I became the antithesis. Perhaps it was inevitable that in my campaign to change Alyona, I had changed myself.

I imploded with loud, shouting admonishments at the slightest provocation. And Alyona, an astute reader of people, obligingly met my presumptions of the worst. Her outbursts became more physically threatening and the potential of her requiring hospitalization held no deterring impact on her behaviors. In fact, she seemed to develop a laissez-faire attitude and seemed freer to do whatever she wanted, as the consequences were of no concern.

I had to replace three doors to her bedroom and acquired some serious skills at patching wallboard. I resisted the urge to paint over the obscenities she had written on every wall using crayon or permanent marker; that would have been futile, as she would have simply redone the work, and scoffed at my attempts to cover it up.

During one of her rages I heard her window shatter. Since she had not screamed in pain, my first thought was that she was climbing onto the roof to escape. I ran out into the forty-degree night and looked up from the yard to see her leaning halfway out of her room.

"See what I did?" she yelled. "Too bad."

She laughed a devilish cackle, while showing off the curtain rod she'd used to break the glass. "You're mean," she yelled down at me. "I hate you." She threw a shard of broken pane onto the roof, then another into the yard. I kept my distance in case she aimed a piece at me. She switched to clothes, however: Bellowing, she tossed shirts, dresses and pants outside. Shoes and books came next.

"Mom, do you want me to go to a safe house?" I heard Alec ask, as I dialed 911. "Yes, Yes," I answered, distracted. I didn't notice that he hustled across the street barefoot and wearing only boxer shorts. I hung up with the police dispatcher and called Judy.

Neighbors began to congregate at the scene and I asked Ed, a neighbor, to accompany me to Alyona's room. Ed is a big man who'd been summoned for help by his daughter, one of my past babysitters, when she'd looked after the kids. I figured he knew what to expect.

Alyona stood calmly in the middle of a room carpeted in glass fragments, her eyes crazed. Freezing air wafted through the glassless window. I crossed my arms in front of me for warmth. Alyona wore only a short-sleeved shirt and sweat pants. She didn't look the least bit cold.

I half-expected her to charge me with one of the many pieces of glass lying at hand. She didn't need a weapon: With a wicked growl, she sprang at me and landed a hard punch on the left side of my face. The shock hurt more than the actual blow, but even so, I was stunned; Ed grabbed her and held her until the police arrived.

"Is anyone hurt? Do you need the rescue squad?" a young sergeant asked.

"No one's injured," I replied, as women officers took Alyona to the living room to talk with her.

"Where's your son?" An officer inquired, having been to our home in the past.

"He's gone to a safe house across the street."

I was confident that by now, Alec was warm, cozy and fast asleep. He liked our neighbors, and felt at home sleeping at their place. He knew that I'd pick him up in the morning, and that in the meantime, Judy and the police would see to my protection and Alyona's well-being.

"No one's at home at the house across the street," I heard the officer tell the sergeant. There was a slight edge to his voice. Obviously, I did not have a clue as to the whereabouts of my son.

"There are several safe houses on the block," Judy immediately responded. "We can just check at each of them. Alec knows all available homes, and he's resourceful enough to knock until he finds someone home."

"Breaking the window is against the law," the officer said, satisfied with Judy's explanation. "Do you want to press charges?"

I looked over at Alyona, who was sitting on the stairs. She and Judy were deeply engaged in conversation.

"Ma'am?" He tried again.

"No," I replied. "No, I don't want to press charges." I was shocked at myself for not answering at once. "You need to Alyona-proof her bedroom," Judy recommended. "It's safer for all of you."

I had resisted the idea of installing my daughter in a prison-like secure room. It felt so removed from parenting. This was a pre-teen girl whom I loved, not a savage beast. She was intelligent and pretty. She could be utterly charming. To lock her up seemed hard-hearted, excessive, contradictory. But, the broken window had decided the issue. Having replaced three doors, many square feet of drywall and now a window, I was listening.

"Although it may not seem so, Alyona is ashamed after the outburst at all the destruction she has caused," Judy told me. "It reinforces her poor self-image that she is a bad person. By preventing the destruction, we can help her learn coping skills without the frequent setbacks brought on by the ravages of her anger."

Our home had to represent a safe refuge for everyone, especially while Alyona was learning better self-control. Take away her fear of destructive or hurtful outcomes, and I might take away a source of her shame.

Silvio and Karen, friends from church, came over to help. An engineer by profession, Silvio could handle fix-it jobs big and small, and did so on their rental property. He and his wife, Karen, spent long hours installing wood paneling on the walls, and carpet over that. A heavy, solid door replaced the hollow one. Plexiglas took the place of glass in the window. I paid them in pizza and beer.

When they finished, the room was virtually indestructible. Silvio demonstrated by kicking the wall with great force. "See," he said, "No hole." He pounded the Plexiglas window with his fist. "And no glass. It is a safe room."

Much to my surprise, Alyona was not offended. As Judy had anticipated, she actually seemed able to better relax. It was now a space to which she retreated without fear of negative consequence. Locked in her room, she could lash out at her demons by imagining them in the door and walls.

She would emerge from such sessions drained and subdued, even tender—and now, I noticed, crying real tears. I also recognized other encouraging signs. "Will you lie down with me until I fall asleep?" she'd ask, then cuddle beside me, arm and leg draped across my body. She was more willing to talk about how she felt, about other options she might have chosen. I sensed that we were on a brink of change. I couldn't help but think that her safe room environment made it seem less risky for her to take chances with changed behavior. Did she feel safer both physically and emotionally? Did that make it possible for her to trust?

Still, there came times when the explosions could not be confined to those four walls, such as the day I got a frantic call from Talia, the kids' sitter who had made the Tennessee trip with us: "Alyona's grabbing the steering wheel and trying to switch the gears," she yelled over the cell phone. "She went bonkers when I told her she couldn't have a soda. Alec's in the backseat. I can't drive this way." I could hear Alyona guffawing in the background.

"Where are you?"

"Near the mall," Talia said, turning from the phone to gasp, "Alyona, stop!" The panic in her voice was unmistakable.

"Go to the Quick Mart," I told her. "I'll meet you there."

I found Talia's car idling near the grassy divide that separated the Quick Mart's parking lot from that of a nearby professional building. The car's windows were closed. I could see Alyona. Even while the car idled, she kept grabbing for the steering wheel, the ignition key and the gear shift. As I watched, she hit the horn several times. "I want a soda," I heard her yell. "I want a soda." She grabbed for the keys.

"Unlock the door so I can get Alyona," I shouted through the glass. "I'll keep her until she calms down. You and Alec go home." Talia pushed the unlock button.

I yanked Alyona out of the car, no doubt to the horror of the small crowd that was now gathering on the sidewalk in front of the store. Alyona kicked and pulled at my grasp on her upper arms.

"You fucking bitch," she spat. "Leave me alone!" She kicked my legs.

"Alyona, pull yourself together," I told her. "There's no need for this behavior." I spoke softly, but was not optimistic that reason or logic would have any impact; I feared that only exhaustion would put the brakes on her defiance.

"I don't have to listen to you, bitch," she barked. "You're not my mother. I hate you."

She suddenly jerked up both of her arms, striking the underside of my forearms with a power that belied her size, snapping my hold on her. She broke for the road. I grabbed her arm; she jerked me towards her, and we both tumbled to the grass. One heel flew off my foot and my multicolored dress whirled around us both as we wrestled on the ground.

"Do you want me to get Dr. Kennedy?" Dodging a head butt, I turned towards the voice. It was the nurse from our family doctor's office, which was in the building next door. She held a salad and a soda she'd just bought at the Quick Mart.

"Please," I grunted while fending off Alyona's swings.

Another voice, deeper: "What's going on here?" A tall, muscular policeman stood over us. Alyona instantly halted her struggle when she saw him, holstered gun on his hip. "Alyona's bipolar," I told the cop in a rush. "She has problems with violence. Police have been to our home a number of times."

The nurse took Alyona, dripping wet with perspiration, to her car. They sat together in its cool. I lurched to my feet. My hose were shredded, and grass stains covered my rumpled dress. My glasses were bent and lay crooked on my nose. I ran my hand through my hair, combing out blades of grass in the process. I was embarrassed to give my name and job title.

Dr. Kennedy arrived on the scene, and quickly and concisely explained Alyona's mental condition to the policeman, who confirmed her history via a radio call to the dispatcher. "Dr. Welch is not a child abuser," Dr. Kennedy told the cop. "Alyona is actually much better than when she first came from Ukraine."

After conferring with his superiors, the officer released us to go home. "I don't want to get any more calls about you," he said as he left.

After six months, Judy delivered, and I was unable to find an in-home therapist to replace her. Although Alyona had made great strides in self-control, there were still moments when I missed Judy's calm, wise presence. One time I summoned the police to my house was especially frightening. Alyona insisted that she be permitted to watch TV while eating dinner in the living room. I was equally insistent that we all sit at the table. She spilled all the food from her plate onto the floor.

"Go to your room," I screamed at her.

"You can't make me," she replied, then made a mad dash for the living room.

Theresa, who was temporarily staying with us, caught hold of her by one wrist. "Listen to your mom," she said, "and go to your room."

Alyona immediately started swinging with her free arm. I wrapped my arms around her chest and yanked her backwards to get her off balance. "Grab her feet," I told Theresa, "and we'll carry her upstairs."

I had the easier end. Kicking ferociously, Alyona was able to get one foot free, but Theresa locked on to the other with great tenacity, despite repeated kicks to her hands. "You motherfuckers," my daughter screeched. "Get your damn hands off of me."

"Alec, go to a safe house," I had the presence of mind to yell.

We staggered upstairs, our grip slippery with sweat, Alyona writhing. She gave a powerful kick to the wall with her free leg, knocking both Theresa and me to our knees, but we held on. When we got to the top of the stairs, Alyona grabbed the railing and pulled with such force that she wrestled free of both of us. She dived for a nook in the hallway, and rolled onto her back. She was now wedged so she could kick at anyone who came near.

"Theresa," I wheezed, "call 911."

Each time I tried to grab her to take her to her room, she kicked me hard in the gut. I tried walking away, hoping she'd calm down—or better yet, go to her room on her own. She didn't budge, and didn't cool off. When I turned away, she kicked at the railing, trying to break through. The thought that she might succeed, and fall down the stairs, scared me.

Theresa talked to her through the railing, trying to distract her as I moved in closer. Alyona was not easily deceived, however; each time, she gave a mighty kick aimed directly for my solar plexus. If I yowled in pain, she heard it as a cry of encouragement

By the time the police arrived I was unable to stand up straight, my abdomen was in such pain. I was certain that my injury was muscular, nothing serious; still, the EMTs insisted on assessing me. They wanted me to be examined at the emergency room, but I refused, as I wanted to be with Alyona for her admission.

"Do you want to press charges this time?" the police asked.

I refused, of course. But an astute paramedic made a comment that lodged in my brain. "There will come a time, Dr. Welch," he said, "when you are going to have to make some tough decisions. You can't go on like this. It's not safe for you or your children."

Dulled by the blaring noise from the television, the lanky brunette draped one leg over the arm of the chair and rested her head on the other large, cushioned arm, staring in the direction of the screen. A husky black-curly haired boy lay snoring on the nearby sofa. Alyona and I stood waiting for her discharge. I clutched the rumpled brown bag containing her three days worth of clothes. I pressed the bag against my chest, clinging to some semblance of normal—everyday clothes for a pre-teen little girl. I tried to insulate myself from the surrounding madness, yet recalled Alyona's stark madness three days before—-her unprompted transformation from giggling young girl to screaming, destructive, violent beast. This was Alyona's fifth admission in three months; I hoped the medication adjustment would prove a magic wand. I wanted, more than anything, to never bring her here again. I had a bit of magic myself that I wanted to try.

In a short while, Alyona and I walked through the massive door, but we were not going home. I had a blanket and small shoe box in the back seat. "We're going to one of your favorite places," I told her when we got to the car.

"Where?" she asked. I wouldn't say. As with the past discharges, Alyona was in a quiet, compliant mood. It seemed she absorbed as much calm from her surroundings as she could, at such times, as if this might somehow gird her against future eruptions. Maybe there was a fear that if she asked too much, she would be dissatisfied with the answer, and her good mood would evaporate.

When we arrived at the entrance gate to the military base, Alyona, who had sat with her head lowered for most of the trip, straightened up and exclaimed, "Oh boy, the beach," her expression brightening into a grin. I drove the short distance to the Officer's Club and parked in an otherwise deserted lot. Grabbing the shoe box and blanket, I said, "OK, let's head to your spot." She was already out of the car and needed no nudging.

We walked a wood-slat causeway over the sand dunes, snaking amid large sprays of salt grass. It was an overcast, blustery day and sand stung our faces; we both instinctively bowed our heads and held our jackets tight. Sea gulls wheeled overhead, and a few followed us from their perch on the wooden rail. Alyona and I walked in silence, as we'd done before; we'd often retreated to the bay, more for spiritual revival than to sun-bathe or frolic in the water (Alyona actually didn't like venturing from shore: "I'm scared," she told me, "because I can't see all the animals in the water").

As soon as we stepped onto the fine white sand, she paused, slowly looked over the vast expanse of water, sucked in a deep chestful of salty air—and smiled. "I see dolphins, mom," she said. I squinted at the water, saw none. Then again, that's not unusual. Alyona has always had a sixth sense about their presence, as if she is able to commune with them. "They're probably very glad to see you," I responded.

Taking our shoes off, we traipsed through deep sand. "Let's put the blanket here," I said, directing us to a firm patch not far from the water. "Let's sit so I can show you something."

We sat. I opened the shoebox. "There's nothing in it," a disappointed Alyona exclaimed. "Aaaah," I said, "but we are going to fill it with some very important things."

"This is a magical box," I continued—-I was relying on a child's innocent acceptance of mystery and all the power attributed to it. "This box can hold all the memories that hurt you, smash them down to pieces and then we can toss them out to the ocean." I hoped I sounded convincing.

"I like that," Alyona said.

I carefully wrapped my hands around Alyona's head and mimed pulling a large quantity of something out, wrapping my arms around it and shoving it into the box. Alyona quickly slammed the lid on top for good measure. I then repeated the motion extracting the pain from her heart. I held the lid tightly to the box as we walked to the water's edge.

I held the box high, "Oh mighty ocean," I cried, "We give you all these things that hurt Alyona. I ask you to carry them far out to sea where they may never return." I knew this was all for show, but I prayed the real magic would be the strength of Alyona's belief in what I was doing. She stood mesmerized by the thrash of the waves, the salty spray on her face, the icy water swirling around our feet.

I opened the box and threw the invisible contents out to sea. I shooed the air to assure any stray bits were propelled far away from us. Alyona kicked at them, chanting, "Go away, go away."

I imagined I was feeding a hungry god, offering Alyona's pain as a sacrifice. "Please, somehow, somewhere, make this help," I thought. As we turned to walk back to the car, I spied a single dolphin's fin offshore.

I can't say that this particular cleansing healed Alyona, but I can say that I never again admitted her to the hospital.

When Alyona lost television privileges for the weekend because she didn't clean her room as promised, she stomped outside and took a brisk walk. When I refused to immediately go to the grocery store to buy what she wanted for dinner, she huffed upstairs to her room, slammed the door and blasted her music as loud as it could go. On one occasion, following a loss of computer privileges, she went outside to the back yard and screamed as loud as she could for a minute. I was hopeful: She was choosing non-destructive responses and was learning the meaning of saying whatever she chose under her breath, but not out loud.

Another valuable trait that I saw emerging was that she shared her insights and thoughts about our disagreements or her blow-ups. With rare exception, I could trust that after a storm, she would, on her own initiative, come to me and start a conversation, "This is what is going on with me right now," she might start. "And this is what I could have done differently...." It didn't mean that the bad behavior didn't happen, mind you, but it sure reminded her that her fits probably weren't the best strategy for getting her way. She was beginning to understand the distinction between feeling an emotion—anger, disappointment, whatever—and expressing that emotion.

On one occasion, while we visited my sister, Robbie, in Orlando, Alyona had her newfound skills put to the test. Robbie had prepared a very nice dinner, going to great pains to include things the children liked. Alyona refused to taste even one green bean.

"Just one, Alyona. It's no big deal." Robbie pleaded. "In our house, the rule is that you at least take a little taste of everything. Sometimes you even learn new things to like."

"I don't care," an emphatic Alyona replied. "I don't want any and I'm not going to taste it." With that she rose from the table and strode out the door into the blackness of the night. To her credit, she went without a word of profanity, and she was using a coping technique that was acceptable at home. But, this being the first time we had visited Robbie at her new home, the neighborhood was a blank to her.

"Alyona, wait," I yelled after her. She disappeared before we could catch her. We divided into teams, inviting neighbors to join in the search. Armed with flashlights, we fanned out through backyards and ruffled bushes. We searched for her for an hour, without success, my own emotions bouncing between fear and anger. At that point, I concluded that we needed more help. "Call the police," I told my sister.

I gave the officers pictures and described her emotional problems. Two cruisers were parked in front of the house. As I was talking to them, Alyona, cocky at having caused such a ruckus, strutted out from behind some bushes. My other sister, Ruth, a special education teacher who had often shared wise counsel, spotted her and snatched her by the arm. Alyona did not resist.

⌒⌒

Alyona was oblivious to how her physical strength had grown as she'd grown. On the way home from church one day she became furious because I nixed her request that we go out to eat. She went from grumpy to shouts to delivering a tremendous kick to the windshield in a matter of seconds. A crack spread at once across the glass.

She was flabbergasted and burst into tears. "I didn't mean to," she wailed. "It was an accident." She had kicked the window in the past without causing damage.

I recalled how the in-home therapist had emphasized to both of us the need for clear, strict boundaries—that there be no breaking of the law and no harming of herself or others. The words of the paramedic—"One of these days you are going to have to make some tough decisions"—haunted me.

"I'm pressing charges for destruction of property," I told Alyona. She was stunned and frightened. In her mind, if she'd intended no harm, she should face no punishment. "That's not fair," she cried. "It was an accident."

"I truly believe that you did not mean to break the window," I said. "But you took the risk by kicking it, so you're responsible for the results." It amounted to a new ratcheted-up level of learning for my daughter. As Judy had put it: "We keep tightening the reins a bit."

The next morning I sat in the courthouse's family services waiting room with a tall, strapping boy who had to waddle, wide-legged, to keep his pants from slipping to his knees. His checkered red boxer shorts peeked out from under his navy blue tee shirt. The shirt was emblazoned with bright red letters reading, "Kill or Be Killed." The slogan was made all the more powerful by a depiction of a knife, dripping blood, that hovered over the words.

A petite teenage girl with purple spiked hair and a black leather outfit bedecked with chains sat two seats away. She had rings in her ears, eyebrows, nose and lip. She chewed her gum vigorously, every so often blowing a small bubble until it popped.

I was definitely overdressed in my suit and heels! As I wrote out the scenario and complaint, I found myself slouching in the chair, feeling guilty. When I turned in the form, I almost apologized.

Dale Holden certainly didn't fit my preconceived notion of a probation officer. His eyes sparkled when he spoke and he had a mischievous grin. He moved with the ease of an athlete. But he was no-nonsense when he spoke to Alyona. "You broke the law," he told her. "And now you have to pay the consequences."

"I didn't mean to break the window," she said. "It was an accident. I'm sorry I did it."

"Doesn't make any difference, so don't waste my time with that argument," he replied. "And you weren't sorry enough to stop the kick." He could be as relentless in his way, as Alyona.

During Mr. Holden's tenure as an in-home therapist and now in the probation system, he had acquired a sense for discerning truth from fiction. He wasted no time confronting Alyona's attempts at manipulation, and refused to let her wallow for over a moment in self-pity or inertia. He was focused, firm and clear on her boundaries and his expectations. The past was no excuse for misbehavior. Consequences, good and bad, would be fair and consistently applied.

Mr. Holden was also personable, quick to praise, an easy conversationalist, and had an engaging presence that both comforted and motivated. Alyona and I needed him. In their weekly sessions, he helped Alyona understand that the court was her last stop.

"There's no begging with the judge," he said. "It's beyond your mom now. You do what the judge says or you go to detention." Alyona focused on his words. She hardly blinked.

"In the courtroom, there's a door to the right of the judge," Mr. Holden told her. "It's behind where the uniformed deputy stands. If the judge thinks you're not trying to change your behaviors or you are not doing what you're supposed to be doing then the officer takes you right then through that door and you go to detention. And your mom or I can't do anything about it."

The lanky teenage boy a few seats away slumped farther down in his chair, legs stretched in front of him. He fiddled with his shirt collar and tie, obviously not accustomed to being dressed up. His lawyer spoke quietly. The boy kept his eyes closed, as if to tune the man out. His mother, though, sat upright on the edge of her seat peering intently into the lawyer's eyes. Her hands were tightly clasped on her lap. A package of tissues sat on the chair beside her. A name was called; the trio rose and followed the deputy into the court room.

In a short while, the door again opened and only the mother exited. "They took my baby," she sobbed. "They took my baby." Alyona turned towards me but said nothing.

"Alyona Welch," the deputy called.

Judge Larry Willis, sitting high on the dais at the front of the room, projected an unchallenged ease with his responsibilities. There were two pedestal podiums positioned on either side of the dais facing the judge. A court-appointed defense lawyer steered Alyona to the one on the left. Instinctively, I followed.

Mr. Holden intercepted me, and steered me to the other podium. "You're the plaintiff," he explained, "and she's the defendant."

It suddenly struck me—late, I know, but this is where it happened— that for purposes of these proceedings, it was a "me versus you" situation. We were not a family unit. Alyona looked so small, alone and vulnerable. I caught her stealing a glance at the door behind the deputy. I wanted to hug her. The ten-foot divide between us seemed insurmountable.

"Are you ready?" The judge asked.

"Yes, sir," I said.

Mr. Holden was persuasive. The judge turned to Alyona. "It's up to you," he told her. "You seem like a smart young girl. Get your behaviors under control and you will do very well."

"Yes, sir," Alyona promised. "I will, sir." The judge ordered community service and continued probation. I felt enormous relief.

Once a week, Alyona worked in a community vegetable garden. She worked in the rain. She worked in the cold. On those days when she balked at working, a simple reminder of the judge's words prompted her to get with the program.

When we periodically appeared before the judge for a report on her progress, Alyona was contrite, respectful and earnest. There were neither excuses from her when she faltered, nor any from me. It was humbling to stand in a stark courtroom, before a black-robed judge sitting tall on the bench, and to have our behavior—my behavior—assessed.

The most profound lesson we both received, I think, was the concept of community standards, and how our family expectation had to mesh with, and stay true to, those of society at large. Alyona learned that she didn't want to be in the court system again. She also began to comprehend the notion that her choices and controls would indeed shape her life. She moved closer to transcending the past in favor of grasping at the future.

This lesson of community standards was pleasantly reemphasized by our "tag team" of after-school sitters. I had decided that the wisest choice for after-school care was right at home. This provided Alyona and Alec with familiar surroundings and comforts, and it avoided the trouble that always brewed when they were in a large group of children.

The "tag team" consisted of three friends who were in their senior year of a home-schooled program. Melissa was the cheerleader of the group, an always positive and energetic blonde receptive to spontaneous ideas—going to get ice cream, taking pictures, playing soccer in the park. Maleka, a native Hawaiian, was the most disciplined and organized of the three and always approached decision-making with logic and reason. Rick was laissez-faire about school, his future and life in general. He loved sports and would just as soon play catch with Alec or Alyona as help them with their homework.

Because each of them offered his own brand of supervision, Alyona and Alec found their after-school hours fun and interesting. And Melissa, Maleka and Rick were good role models, consistent in the respect, kindness, adaptability and caring they demonstrated, the honesty and citizenship they stressed. Alyona and Alec were not resistant to learning as it seemed more engagement than lesson. They were subtly growing in their concepts of family, community and values.

Tradition at Alyona's school held that younger students lined the halls as graduating fifth-graders walked out for the final time, accompanied by cheers, applause, hugs and tears. Alyona didn't want to walk. "I don't want to leave you," she told Ms. Weaver, tears streaming down her cheeks. "Please don't make me go."

"You'll be fine Alyona," Ms. Weaver said. "You're ready for middle school. And you can come visit me any time."

Ms. Weaver held Alyona close and together they walked the corridor. When they got to the exit, I slid beside Alyona and Ms. Weaver quietly stepped away. Together, Alyona and I walked through the door symbolizing her ascension to middle school.

Alyona cried because she was saying goodbye to Ms. Weaver. I cried because Alyona had come to care so much about someone that her heart broke at their farewell. Alyona's heart had softened. There was no manipulation, no protections. She was crying because she cared, not because she was out to gain something. I blessed each tear as I kissed Alyona's cheeks and held her close.

Chapter 18

Desire is a powerful motivator. Alyona desired to be normal. She desperately wanted to do well in school, to make friends and to fit in with everyone else. She spent hours working on homework, frustrated by what she saw as academic ineptness. The past emotional eruptions, and the time at The Bridges, had left Alyona with a major handicap—she was several years behind in reading skills. Her efforts at success were not being rewarded. Her grades were dismal and she felt stupid and embarrassed.

How do you convince a young girl that she is bright and intelligent when she can't read like her peers or perform well on tests? The new, evolved Alyona also was driven to behave properly. She was the model of politeness and compliance. It required her full concentration and physical forbearance. She was physically and emotionally exhausted by the effort. She was following a course that would ultimately only reinforce her feelings of inadequacy.

Alyona regularly spent time with Traci, the new in-home therapist assigned to her as a condition of the probation. Traci was perky, effervescent and petite. Her mere presence conjured up memories of high school cheerleaders and football games. Alyona described her as "cool" and "hip." Yet Traci also was bright, politely forthright and obviously very experienced and competent in dealing with behavioral problems in tweens. Traci tried to get Alyona to understand "normal" as permitting mistakes but simply adapting to them, or correcting them in a healthy way. But Alyona saw any mistake as failure.

Ultimately it was seemingly minor incidents that pushed Alyona over the edge, such as an arrogant and sassy young girl who was disrespectful to the teacher. Alyona, ostensibly in support of the teacher, became even more obnoxious towards the student. "Who the fuck do you think you are? Listen to the teacher," she shouted at the girl. Perhaps Alyona was raging at an earlier version of herself. Regardless, it was Alyona who was called out of the classroom and suspended.

At times Alyona refused to do class assignments because she didn't understand it, or in deference to chatting with friends. Her undoing was that she could rationalize misbehavior but not imperfection. To cover her embarrassment at being corrected, Alyona would resort to insubordinate behaviors directed at her ED teacher, Ms. Kennedy.

In that strange paradox of human behaviors, Alyona would strike out at the person most dear to her heart. Ms. Kennedy was a gentle and nurturing spirit whose kindness might seem folly to a manipulative student. But her resolute belief in Alyona and focus on helping her improve had created an inexorable bond between them. Alyona knew she was safe, so she verbally attacked. And with each episode, Alyona fell further behind academically.

"Maybe I made a major mistake letting you move ahead to sixth grade when you were so far behind in reading skills," I vented while driving Alyona to school. "If you can't do the work, then I'll just move you back to fifth."

Progress reports had just been sent home and Alyona's were appalling. We were both angry, but for different reasons. "You've just given up on me," Alyona said. "You said you would never quit."

Suddenly, I knew the real issue. "I've never given up on you, Alyona," I told her. "The problem is that you have given up on yourself. You have forgotten to believe in yourself."

There was silence, except for a public radio program on the war in Iraq. She stared directly at me and through me at the same time. In her eyes I saw anger and fear replaced by introspection. Her muscles softened. Her pupils were enlarged and I could almost see my reflection. She was looking at me, but the real images she saw and felt were deep within herself.

At that moment, she let the tethers of "orphanage Alyona" fall to the ground without resistance. She assimilated the Alyona whom she had kept hidden even from herself. There was no exhilaration, but rather a quiet and welcome surrender.

For the first time in her life she understood that the power was within her. She only had to believe. This moment of epiphany was a mind-boggling milestone.

"You're right," was her simple reply.

Alyona truly began to enjoy herself and enjoy a much more relaxed demeanor. She developed genuine friendships, raised her reading skills by three grades and brought all her grades to respectable passes. She became a more confident person who enjoyed her own company.

That she'd turned a corner was evident one summer when Alyona and Alec were campers at the YMCA camp where I volunteered as camp doctor. On talent night Alyona walked to the stage and eagerly took the hand microphone. She began to sing.

> Because of you
> I find it hard to trust not only me, but everyone
> around me
> Because of you
> I am afraid

Her voice was timid and soft, not a dynamic stage presence. Her eyes were closed and she was belting the words internally to herself. She wasn't just singing; she was stroking each word to feel their full meaning. The confession of fear was for both her and me. Now she was ready to move beyond it. She was ready to trust. She was ready to really be a family with

Alec and me. My heart choked at the message. But I felt tall and proud of her delivery of the song and her delivery of herself to the world.

What really brought my tears was seeing her entire cabin swarm on her with hugs and screams of joy after the song. She was selected by the staff for a Sunshine award for her positive spirit and leadership and her cabin was the honor cabin.

She now knows normal. She knows joy. She knows family and friends. She believes in herself.

Alec experienced the same transformations. At the YMCA camp he excelled on the alpine obstacle climbing tower and made a perfect score on his Standards of Learning tests at school. He reveled in reading fact books and in sharing his discoveries.

I had the easy part of this journey. I simply had to endure, to love and to believe. Alyona and Alec had to change the innermost foundations of their responses to life. They had to have faith in strangers and in an even stranger style of life. They had to tear out of the taut and sturdy cover that had encased their spirits. They had to be resilient for no other reason than that I said I loved them and it would be all right.

I'm reminded of a time when we were at the beach and seagulls circled us in the air and on the ground, diving and pecking crumbs of food on the boardwalk. They were raucous in their protests when we refused to share our lunches, or when other birds got to the crumbs first. A few of them hovered inches from our faces demanding attention.

And then, without ado, they quit the fuss, glided over the beach to the water, and settled on the waves, contentedly riding the crests.

"Look, mom," Alyona said, "sea-eagles,"

I looked down at her, and marveled that when you have kids, all the world can seem a metaphor.

Epilogue

"Well, King, they're teenagers now," I murmured. "Did you think we ever would make it?" A warm sweater, a glass of Riesling and my bespectacled porch friend encouraged reflection. "It's not exactly as I imagined it."

Indeed, there'd been nothing textbook about my years in motherhood. But then, I've rarely done things by the book. In medicine and public health it has always seemed that the bizarre gravitates my way, the cases and situations that weren't in the book or defied neat and organized solutions. Which is no complaint. I bore easily. I get an adrenaline rush from the unexpected and unusual. I love the challenge of multi-tasking and creative problem-solving. I'm energized by the words, "We have a problem and no idea how to handle it." My brain kicks into high gear, I consume data, analyze, gather ideas from many other involved parties, discuss alternatives and then implement a potential solution, always with the caveat that if it doesn't work we'll find another that does. It's not as fulfilling to simply apply a boiler-plate answer. I truly don't try to rebel against tradition; I just try to resolve the problem the best way possible. Yet, I have been told on many an occasion, "You think so far outside of the box that I'm not even sure you know where the box is." Well, Alyona and Alec certainly weren't in the box, so I guess it was only fitting that we should become a family.

"I confess, though, King," I sighed, "I was a bit naïve about how hard it would be."

That long-ago July when I flew to Ukraine to choose my children, I had envisioned language problems, a few temper tantrums, confusion, maybe depression, but certainly not the grand tempest that occurred. I'd thought the biggest problem with sitters would be the logistics of scheduling—not the reality of assuring their safety. The children would learn the language in a year, I figured, and fit right into suburban American life.

I'd had no concept of how public our family life would become. By nature, I'm an introvert and a rather private person. But there's absolutely no way I could have done it by myself. Everyone else probably recognized that truth sooner than I, as evidenced by the mass of support I received from friends, my family, the neighborhood, my church, my coworkers and the children's schools. It was a new experience for me to receive so much help, and I admit that I felt a bit awkward about it at first, and took a while to offer thanks without making it sound like an apology. Then I realized we were going to drown if I didn't set pride aside and clamor for every available resource. I learned not to be embarrassed about anything. I learned that most people are eager to help if only you ask them. I learned to forget about my image and preconceived ideas about parenting and to just focus on the kids and solve our problems, one day, one hour or one minute at a time. I learned that thinking outside the box applied to home as well as work. I learned to be humbled.

I also developed a new mantra: "Don't waste a mistake. Learn from it, solve it and move on." This philosophy saved me a lot of self-flagellation. It also gave the kids permission to make mistakes without embarrassment or fear of reprimand. All three of us had steep learning curves. A lot of outbursts were thwarted, or actually converted into fun moments, when I could pause long enough to repeat this mantra. It entailed a bit of a paradigm shift for me, in that it focused more on the learning process than the actual outcome.

I took a sip of wine, pondering the impact of being single has had on my parenting experience. The most obvious, of course, is that I had no back-up, no one to whom I could turn at desperate moments and say, "I can't do this anymore, you take over." I could never walk away from the situation. No matter how exhausted, physically and emotionally, I had to keep plodding forward—-had to stand strong in combat, sometimes literally. I had to resist the temptation to just sit on the floor and cry. Somehow, from somewhere, a new surge of energy would permeate my being and I'd hang in there, outlasting Alyona and Alec. But I have to say, it sure would have been nice to have been able to walk away sometimes.

But there actually were some benefits. I never had to debate or argue with someone about what to do about the children's behavior. Right or wrong, mine was the first and final word, and what I decided was immediately implemented. I might debate with myself about it later, or run it past friends, and both might affect my future decisions, but I never hesitated in the heat of a meltdown—-I just did what, on the spot, made the most sense to me. Period. The kids knew who was in charge and couldn't play one against the other.

That's not to say that I wouldn't have welcomed input and suggestions. It's a scary feeling to be making so many major decisions without the benefit of insights from others; after all, there are no established recipes for what to do under the circumstances I faced. And there was no one else to blame when I really messed up and responded in a manner that actually made matters worse—-that escalated the kids' negative behavior or was contrary to how I had acted to a similar situation in the past. It was hard to be consistent, and that could be confusing for the children. More humbling experiences.

I did teach them, though, to love and to laugh. They have goals now—to be a photographer or graphic designer for Alyona, a math teacher for Alec. They're unafraid of life. And, unlike most teenagers, we can talk about anything. They have a sharp wit and sometimes self-deprecating humor. Most of the time, they're not afraid to be honest, even if there are consequences. And Alyona's insights are profound. Academically, they're just beginning to hit their stride.

Love, though, was never actually one of my objectives for them. I wanted to provide them an environment where they could feel safe; where they could thrive and believe in themselves. I wanted them to be able to enjoy life and to have goals they could achieve. I wanted them to heal. Alyona, who is prone to put things in perspective, reminds me, that in the end, only they could heal themselves. No one could do it for them. The best I could do was to provide an environment conducive to their healing. I believe I did that. But love was left to fate.

And love happened. I know it every day. Even in simple ways.

Like early school-day mornings when a bleary-eyed Alyona, wearing her multi-colored striped pajamas, ambles downstairs to the kitchen for breakfast. She silently and slowly walks towards me, her ruffled hair covering one eye. She wraps her arms around me, snuggles her head in the crook of my neck and says, "I love you, Mommy." The eggs can wait.

Or when Alec and I attend an ice hockey game. With hot dogs in hand, we walk the aisle to our seats. Several inches taller than I, he casually and unabashedly drapes his lanky arm across the back of my shoulders, gives me one of his captivating grins and says, "Mom, I love you." My heart melts.

Yes, love happened.

*Alyona—Shaving
cream escapade, 2004*

Alec—Orphanage, 1999

Alec and Alyona—2012

Alec and Alyona in Kiev, 1999

Arrival in the States
1999

Alyona—Self Portrait
2012

Alex—Eagle Scout
2012

Every worthwhile accomplishment, big or little, has its stages of drudgery and triumph: a beginning, a struggle, and a victory.

—Mahatma Gandhi

A child's hope relies on our steadfast belief in them; no matter what, we will be by their side.

—Anonymous

Author

Nancy M. Welch, MD, MHA, MBA, FAAP, FACPM has been a Health Director in Virginia since 1976 and since 1987 has been Health Director of the Chesapeake Health Department. Following graduation from Lynchburg College, she earned her MD from Duke Medical School and then completed Pediatric Residency at the University of Colorado. A Masters in Health Administration was obtained from the University of Colorado and a Masters in Business Administration from Old Dominion University. She is board certified both in Pediatrics and Preventive Medicine. She is an adjunct faculty at both the Eastern Virginia Medical School and the EVMS-ODU Masters in Public Health program. She has published numerous professional articles and is a frequently invited speaker. She has been the recipient of several local and state awards for public health and community service and is often interviewed on public health matters by the media (newspaper, television, radio). For almost 14 years she volunteered as a Pediatrician, first with the Camp Easter Seal summer program and then with the YMCA summer program. Having explained the alphabet soup behind her name and her professional experience, she would now say that, except for her basic knowledge of behavioral and developmental issues, all this academic background had very little relevance to the parental challenges conveyed in this book.

More important were traits learned while growing up in a family of five children to parents with limited income but an abundance of family commitment, sense of humor and a well-grounded focus on the real values and priorities of life. Birthed second between the two boys taught her doggedness, patience, adaptability and immunity to intimidation. It is these qualities, bolstered by a plethora of support and a steadfast belief in the redeemable strength of these children that has enabled a happy ending to their chronicle of adjustment and conquest of what some would have labeled insurmountable hurdles.

Her strong faith helped shape her abiding dedication to bring her family through tumultuous times to a celebration of the wonderfully unique, clever, insightful and loving persons who emerged as a part of her life and of the world.

Innately a very private person, she breeched her protective walls to share her family's battles and vulnerabilities in a personal and intimate manner. She does it to provide inspiration and hope for all parents with children with behavioral problems and to implore such families to seek help and not be stifled by shame or embarrassment. She does it to beseech communities to hear those cries for help and to respond. Most importantly, she does it out of respect, admiration and awe for her children who have clamored from the depths of savagery to an exciting realm of decency and normalcy. They are her heroes.

The author is available for tours and seminars
and can be contacted at:

Nancy M. Welch, WELFAM, LLC
Nmwelch@hotmail.com

The author will donate 10% of book sales at non-bookstore events to an agreed upon charitable organization that focuses on prevention of child abuse or strengthening services for children with mental illness.

Printed in the USA
CPSIA information can be obtained
at www.ICGtesting.com
JSHW020045140324
59158JS00004B/295

9 781614 486961